OTHER TITLES OF INTEREST FR

The Motivating Team Leader

Skills of Encouragement: Bringing Out the Best in

The New Leader: Bringing Creativity and Innovation to the Workplace

Real Dream Teams: Seven Practices Used by World-Class Team Leaders to Achieve Extraordinary Results

Leadership by Encouragement

What Is, Is: Encouraging Yourself to Accept What You Can't Change and to Change What You Can

Creating Productive Organizations

Team Building: A Structured Learning Approach

Organization Teams: Building Continuous Quality Improvement

Teams in Government: A Handbook for Team-Based Organizations

Reengineering Performance Management: Breakthroughs in Achieving Strategy Through People

The High Cost of Low Morale...and What to Do About It

Reengineering the Training Function: How to Align Training with the New Corporate Agenda

Mastering the Diversity Challenge: Easy On-the-Job Applications for Measurable Results

For more information about these titles call, fax or write:

St. Lucie Press
2000 Corporate Blvd., N.W.
Boca Raton, FL 33431-9868

TEL (561) 994-0555 • (800) 272-7737
FAX (800) 374-3401
E-MAIL information@slpress.com
WEB SITE http://www.slpress.com

S^t_L

The Sky
Is Not
The Limit

Breakthrough Leadership

by Dr. Bart Barthelemy

$$S{}^{t}_L$$

St. Lucie Press
Boca Raton, Florida

Phone: (561) 994-0555
E-mail: information@slpress.com
Web site: http://www.slpress.com

S$_L^t$

Published by
St. Lucie Press
2000 Corporate Blvd., N.W.
Boca Raton, FL 33431-9868

TABLE OF CONTENTS

PREFACE

It was October 1963 when I rolled into Dayton, Ohio. I had burned out the brakes of my 1959 Buick coming over the mountains of West Virginia from Cambridge, Massachusetts, and I was searching for Wright-Patterson Air Force Base. Surely, the world's largest research and development complex would be easy to locate. But I couldn't find it, and I was afraid to drive around any longer because of the brakes. So I stopped at this little diner to ask for directions.

Everything I had was in the car: my two Air Force uniforms that had taken all of the cash advance that the Air Force had sent me, my Air Force commission, my orders to report to Wright-Patterson Air Force Base as a nuclear research officer, and a half-finished draft of my master's thesis that I owed the MIT Department of Nuclear Engineering by December of that year. At the time, my world was centered on getting to the base to work on nuclear propulsion technology for the Air Force. I had graduated with a degree in chemical engineering from MIT in June of 1962 and received my commission into the Air Force a day later. Unfortunately, the Air Force had no interest in chemical engineering (they told me that if I stayed in chemical engineering, they would transfer me to the Army), so they asked me to stay on at MIT to get a master's degree in nuclear engineering. They paid the tuition and some of my expenses, but they wanted me to finish in a year. The year was up, and I was headed for my first real job. At this point, I was frazzled, tired, broke, and lost, but I was excited about my new career in the Air Force. I had always wanted to spend some of my life in government service, and I really wanted to apply my new knowledge in science and engineering to something worthwhile. And what could be more exciting and worthwhile to an MIT graduate than nuclear aircraft propulsion?

I walked up to the counter in the diner, asked the waitress for directions (she thought she knew where it was), and was about to leave when I glanced at a copy of that day's paper on the counter. Sprawled across the front page, in huge letters, was the headline: "Air Force Cancels Nuclear Aircraft Program—All nuclear work at Wright-Patterson to stop." Wonderful, now what? Maybe they'll want me to get another degree. No way. Maybe I should transfer to the Army. No, there was something glamorous about the Air Force. Well, I made my way to the base, checked into the Visiting Officers' Quarters, and contemplated what would happen to me, the has-been nuclear research officer, when I reported in the next day.

Wright-Patterson is the largest Air Force base in the country. It occupies a significant part of the Dayton area, employs about 40,000 people, and is responsible for tens of billions of dollars in federal funds and about a billion dollars in research and development (R&D). How come I couldn't find this place? I was really beginning to wonder if five years at MIT had not damaged my brain. But it really didn't matter, since I now had no meaningful job in the Air Force. I reported to the R&D center at 06:30 hours, ready to salute anyone with anything but gold bars on his shoulders. The gate was closed; the base didn't open until 7 A.M. When I finally got in, I had to wait until 9 A.M. to see my reporting official. I couldn't salute him; he was a civilian. He then introduced me to his supervisor, who was a civilian too. It took me four introductions before I could finally salute somebody. He was the colonel in charge of the whole place. After giving him my best ROTC salute, he told me, "We don't salute around here," shook my hand, and asked if I had any thoughts about what I could do at the R&D laboratories now that nuclear engineering was out.

So began my research career with the Air Force Research and Development Center at Wright-Patterson Air Force Base in Dayton, Ohio. Despite that crazy start, my Air Force assignment turned out to be a great experience. After my four years as an officer (they kept me as a nuclear research officer even though I worked as an electrical engineer), I stayed on as a civilian Air Force employee

From this point, I feel identify with the idea of research and manager

and broadened my R&D career with some research in other fields. Amazingly, there was even some chemical engineering to do. I worked, quite satisfied, for six more years as a scientist, engineer, and technologist, picking up a Ph.D. along the way in, yes, nuclear engineering. They said it would help me in the future. And then it happened, that inevitable decision point which confronts almost every engineer, almost every professional: the opportunity to become a "manager."

When this happens, you get lots of advice. Everyone who is still an engineer tells you that by accepting, you sell your soul to the devil. But every manager tells you it's the only game in town, the way to the top, the chance for big money (in the government, salaries are never big, but managers do get a little more), and the opportunity to make a real difference. I loved doing research, and I had some great times. I even came up with some new ideas. Some of the teams I was on actually produced innovations that might be labeled breakthroughs. But more about that later. I was really happy as a researcher, but the lure of the unknown, the promised omnipotence of a first-level supervisory position, and the obvious glamour of being a civil service bureaucrat was just too much. I succumbed and became an R&D manager.

It seemed simple enough. Before I did research; now I would supervise people who did research. Before I had to go to managers for help and permission; now I gave permission and helped people do research. Unfortunately, or maybe fortunately, I did not become the manager of my own group. I was made the supervisor of a group that did research in space solar energy, an area foreign to me and certainly not one to which I could apply my vast, if untapped, knowledge of nuclear engineering. My intuition told me that if I could learn all about space solar energy, I would become a great manager of this group. Wrong. No one in the group wanted any help. Then I thought that I could really make a contribution by getting to be a buddy with the guys in the space solar energy group. Wrong. They were not interested in being pals; engineers and scientists are not the most outgoing professionals in the world. No matter what I thought would work, it didn't. It was clear after several months that being a manager was going to be a lot different from being a researcher. All my life (by then I was 30) I had dealt with what scientists call "linear systems"—like the business of science and engineering, nuclear particles, stuff like that. When you do something to a linear system, you can predict how it will respond. If you do the same thing to the same linear system, it responds in the same way every time. It was becoming really obvious to me that I was now dealing with some very nonlinear systems—people. These guys never responded consistently to me. How could I manage them if I couldn't predict their behavior? How could I help them if they didn't want me to? How could I add value if they generally saw me as an obstacle or barrier to their work?

So began my management career in the Air Force Research and Development Center at Wright-Patterson Air Force Base in Dayton, Ohio. Despite this second crazy start, my management career also turned out to be a great experience. I became a pretty good manager. I learned how to organize and plan, to coordinate and communicate, to direct and supervise, and to control and evaluate. They sent me to supervisory schools and management schools; then to advanced management schools and leadership schools; finally to executive management schools; and after about ten years, there were no more schools left to attend. It reminded me of my wonderful education in nuclear engineering. I knew that some-day all of this management schooling would pay off. Fortunately for me, I kept getting promoted, so the management challenges got greater: group supervisor to branch chief, branch chief to division manager, and division manager to laboratory director—more people, more money, more research, more power. Now lieu-tenants with gold bars would come in to me, they would salute, I would shake their hands, and together we would try to figure out what they might do in the Air Force research community. Strangely enough, some of them were nuclear engineers, and we still didn't have any nuclear engineering work to give them. During those years, I was involved with some outstanding groups that did some exceptional things, some of which you might even call break-throughs. I learned how to manage, and I learned that manage-ment was important. I also learned that, like people, management was also a nonlinear system. Sometimes, a particular kind of man-agement worked with a particular group of people. But sometimes it didn't and rarely did it work all the time. After about ten years of management, I knew that I didn't know everything about manage-ment, but I was convinced that by applying the fundamental principles of this profession, I could "manage." But was that enough? "Managing" began to feel like "getting by." Given the resources, the people, and the time, my job became one of making sure that nothing would go wrong on the way to achieving the goals. Most of my contribution came in watching what was happening and not letting things get too far out of control. Surely there were more exciting and interesting roles to play in the business that I was in. For a while, I really felt that the only way to contribute was to go back into the research world and become a scientist or engineer once again. That certainly would have been an interesting move, but it didn't seem like the best use of my experience or my talents.

Somewhat as an avocation, I began studying and investigating the business of innovation and creativity. I took every course that I could find and read most of the literature on creativity. Several of us in the Dayton area even formed a nonprofit organization called "Creativity-80s." This opened a path to meet and work with some leaders in the business of innovation, like Edward de Bono, Rosabeth Moss Kanter, Tom Peters, Roger van Oech, Gifford Pinchot, and the folks from the Creativity Centers in Buffalo and Greensboro. My personal search for a creative contribution, along with my duties as an R&D manager, took me down two roads which eventually merged into the idea that I call "Breakthrough Leadership."

. The journey into creativity led to the development of a series of workshops conducted over the past ten years for a wide variety of individuals and organizations. The focus of these workshops has been on high-performance teams, their innovative contributions, and the leadership aspects of these experiences. Over 20,000 individuals from high school students to Fortune 100 CEOs, from church groups to federal government workers, from young people to seniors, and people from almost every walk of life, profession, and interest were involved in these encounters. The goals were to share our high-performing creative experiences, discuss the characteristics of the experiences, and learn to utilize these characteristics in the creation and leadership of our organizations. From this endeavor came an abbreviated book on "High Performance" and the concept that *purposeful focus, integration of strengths, creative opportunity,* and a *spirit of excitement* are at the core of high performance. More importantly, thousands of real-life breakthrough experiences were examined in terms of what really happens when people and teams achieve breakthrough objectives. Not surprisingly, the same characteristics are at the core of all of the experiences, and these form the basis for this writing.

Simultaneously, my Air Force management career provided me with an opportunity to both observe and apply these principles in a setting that depended on creativity and breakthroughs—high-tech research and development. During the same ten-year period, I was involved in three very different assignments in the Air Force R&D world. The first was as the managing director of a 400-person R&D laboratory responsible for the advanced development of jet engines. The task was to focus hundreds of millions of dollars of R&D effort in industry and government in order to achieve continued growth in a critical national industry. The second assignment occurred in the mid-80s when the Air Force leadership created the position of Technical Director (now called Chief Scientist) for its billion-dollar R&D complex at Wright-Patterson Air Force Base. While the word "director" appeared in that position title, the job really involved guiding the efforts of the aerospace industry and the government laboratories into the future. My two years in that position gave me a wonderful opportunity to observe the strategic direction of the aerospace industry, its strengths and weaknesses, and the pockets of really brilliant work in this industry. Fortunately, I was also able to work with my counterparts in other industries such as electronics, automobiles, and consumer products to gain some insight into their successes and challenges.

Nine years ago, another job opportunity led me to a quite different activity—that of directing the National Aero-Space Plane (NASP) program. While some aspects of the previous two positions carried over to the NASP assignment, it really has been a very different and fascinating experience. Perhaps the most focused R&D program ever conducted by the United States, NASP is an attempt by thousands of people to make good on a promised breakthrough, the technical development of an airplane that will take off and land at conventional airports, achieve speeds of 17,000 miles per hour, fly around the world in about two hours, and deliver people and payloads into space.

These three experiences have cumulatively taught me some tough lessons about what does and doesn't work in trying to manage creative organizations to achieve breakthroughs. Over the past decade, I've witnessed and, in some cases, assisted in misdirected failures to achieve breakthroughs. I am sure that there were times when the management and leadership (and that includes me) were as much a part of the problem as a part of the solution. Overall, those three organizations' batting average in achieving real breakthroughs was lower than I would have liked to have seen, and I know that we made some dumb mistakes along the way. But (and this is what has driven me to this endeavor) there were some great breakthroughs, and there were some terrific experiences, and there were some great insights into the leadership of breakthrough teams.

Perhaps the greatest revelation was that there is a way to manage for breakthroughs. From both sides of my career, teaching and managing, that message came through loud and clear. The learnings and teachings provided the model, and the practice and the profession provided the data. Managers and leaders can be effective at moving their organizations to breakthrough. There are techniques and approaches that work and work consistently. The process of innovation and high performance is not random or haphazard. I'm convinced that the limitations that we set for our teams and the barriers that get in the way of achieving breakthroughs can be overcome by appropriate leadership techniques. Obviously, there are some natural and God-given limits to what we can achieve, but they are well beyond what we perceive as the limits of our organizations. The sky is not the limit, not for airplanes, not for this planet, not for our organizations, and not for any of us.

Acknowledgments

This book represents one of the great adventures of my life. It started in the early 60s and has really never stopped for the past thirty years. The adventure involved thousands of people in hundreds of settings, and it is impossible for me to thank every one of these people for the tremendous inspiration and wisdom that they gave me over those years. All I can hope is that I somehow acknowledged their help at the time and that they each know that they are a very important part of this work. There are a few very special individuals, however, that I want to thank personally because without their love and guidance, this book could not have been written.

For their part in the adventure, I feel a very great sense of gratitude:

- to Marge, for being with me during the entire adventure and for showing me what the greatest breakthroughs in life really are.

- to Karen, Kristen, and Kim, for being the greatest breakthroughs in my life.

- to my mother, who, at 89, is still living the adventure with commitment.

- to all my mentors, especially Marc Dunnam, Bill Heiser, Bart Krawetz, General Mike Loh, Scott Crossfield, and Dan Quayle, for their challenging attitudes.

- to all of my partners, especially Jane Glover, Roger Fortman, Doug Allen, Bonnie Kasten, Ron Greene, Jane Boucher, Don Weatherby, Carol Shaw, Mary Gail Biebel, Charlie Smith, the NASP gang, the OTTO's, the IDEAs, and the Creativity- 80 team, for their collaboration and friendship.

- to all my special friends, like Bert Allen, Dick Honneywell, Tom Mahefkey, Barry Waldman, Ted W+12, and all the others who put up with me.

- to all those wonderful leaders, like Norm Augustine, Phil Bouchard, Jim Treadway, and Jim Purvis, who have inspired me in so many ways.

and to Don Quixote of La Mancha, who let me dream the impossible dream.

ABOUT THE AUTHOR

Dr. Bart Barthelemy is currently the Director of Training and Education for Universal Technology Corporation in Dayton, Ohio, where he is responsible for the development of corporate training and education programs and services. He is also a founding member of Taos Laboratories of Santa Fe, New Mexico, where he serves as the Director of the Leadership Laboratory and as the co-leader of the FutureSpace Project.

Dr. Barthelemy is also a partner in the Best Yet Company of London, England, and Aspen, Colorado, as well as Innovation Development Associates, based in Dayton, Ohio, and Palm Beach, Florida. For the past fifteen years, he has worked with senior leaders from IBM, ALCOA, General Motors, Westin Hotels, NCR Corporation, AT&T, Westinghouse, Rockwell, United Technologies, American Greeting Cards, General Foods, MIT, Carnegie-Mellon, UCLA, and the U.S. Air Force.

Dr. Barthelemy served as the Director of the Air Force's Training Systems Product Group, the Director of the National Aero-Space Plane Program, and the Technical Director of the Air Force's Wright Laboratories. In these positions, he was responsible for over ten billion dollars of R&D in the leading-edge fields of virtual reality, modeling and simulation, hypersonic aerodynamics, advanced propulsion, and systems engineering. During his senior executive experience, he led government teams of several thousand people and directed even larger industrial teams.

Dr. Barthelemy has bachelor's and master's degrees in engineering from MIT and a Ph.D. in nuclear physics from Ohio State

University. He has published over 250 papers and conducted over 1,000 workshops. He is the recipient of the National Space Trophy, the Golden Knight Award, and the President's Distinguished Rank Award. He has published two books, *High Performance* and *The Sky Is Not the Limit*, both on breakthrough leadership.

For additional information, please contact Dr. Barthelemy at Universal Technology Corporation, 513-426-8530; Taos Laboratories, 800-982-6799; or Innovation Development Associates, 513-253-6778.

CHAPTER 1

Breakthroughs

Mach 25

Less than a century ago, two inventors from Dayton, Ohio, began playing with the idea of powered flight. They studied the works of earlier balloon and glider flyers and then conceived experiments that they carried out in their bicycle shop to understand how such a concept might work. They challenged each other and, with the help of their sister, accumulated enough information and resources to build the first airplane. Because of the favorable winds and geography, the first powered flight of their aircraft took place in Kitty Hawk, North Carolina, several hundred miles from

Dayton. At great risk and far away from home, Orville Wright, with the help of his brother Wilbur, flew the first airplane for a distance of 120 feet on December 17, 1903. On that day, the airplane was born, and a major breakthrough occurred that would have an enormous impact on mankind and his movement on this planet. Many claim that the airplane is the greatest breakthrough of the 21st century since it has affected, more than any other invention, how our civilization has evolved over the past 100 years.

The 1903 flight of the Wright brothers' airplane achieved a speed of only a few miles per hour. It took the two inventors six years to improve on their aircraft so that it could fly at speeds approaching sixty miles per hour, slightly less than the speed that we now limit automobiles to for highway driving. Once the Wrights paved the way, many other people started working with airplanes, and within ten years of the first flight, an entire community had been created. That community would lead to an industry spurred on by the unique capabilities that the airplane offered the military during World War I.

After the war, great progress was made in aerodynamics and in the development of lightweight materials, reciprocating engines, and flight controls. A wide variety of aircraft, for both commercial and military purposes, were built and flown in the 20s and 30s. World War II forced a major expansion of the airplane industry and also brought another breakthrough which would change airplanes forever—the turbojet engine. Discovered almost simultaneously in England by Sir Frank Whittle and in Germany by Hans J.P. von O'Hain, it would later prove crucial in allowing the airplane to maintain supersonic speeds. Forty-four years after the airplane was invented, using a Reaction Motors rocket engine to power the aircraft, Chuck Yeager broke the sound barrier in the Bell X-1 and achieved what aeronautical engineers refer to as Mach 1, the speed of sound. Once that barrier had been broken, the world entered the supersonic age. Mach 2 (two times the speed of sound) airplanes were built and flown in less than a decade, and the feasibility of useful military and commercial supersonic aircraft was established. During the sixties, three aircraft were investigated which opened up some new regimes in high-speed flight. The Lockheed Skunk Works designed, fabricated, and flew a Mach

3 aircraft in less than 27 months, the SR-71 Blackbird, which saw service in the Air Force until 1990. The Supersonic Transport (SST) program began with the goal of achieving a commercial supersonic airliner that would fly at least twice the speed of sound. Although the U.S. effort on the SST was later cancelled, the program provided the incentive for the Anglo-French joint venture that led to the supersonic Concorde, which is still flying. And in 1965, Scott Crossfield and several other test pilots flew a rocket-powered aircraft called the X-15 to a speed of Mach 6.8. That flight opened up the hypersonic era and, coupled with the advances being made in missile and rocket technology, paved the way for manned space flight and concepts like the Space Shuttle.

By 1983, only eight decades after the Wrights' first flight, airplanes had come a long way. The military routinely flew supersonic fighters and bombers, commercial jet flights typically hovered just under the speed of sound, and hypersonic flight had been demonstrated. Nevertheless, it looked like the end of the line; the sky seemed to have a limit. Flying in the atmosphere at speeds much greater than Mach 3 proved to be extremely challenging. At higher speeds, airplanes had to be fabricated with materials that could take the high temperatures of hypersonic flight and still be light enough for aircraft structural considerations. Fuels had to be much more efficient than the usual kerosene, and the engines required for hypersonic flight were well beyond the state-of-the-art turbojet engines. In order to get to space, the rocket launchers, like Saturn and Atlas, which powered Apollo and Mercury, got out of the atmosphere as soon as possible. Even the Space Shuttle only used the atmosphere on its return to earth. Airplanes seemed to have reached the limits of their materials and propulsion capabilities, and it looked like very high speed flight was not in the cards. Breakthrough after breakthrough had given us ever-increasing speeds, taken us from first flight to Mach 1 in forty years, and routinely allowed Mach 2 flight during the next forty years. But flight above Mach 3 didn't seem feasible. Well, the scientists and engineers who predicted that limitation were wrong.

In 1983, the genesis for a very high speed hypersonic vehicle occurred, once again, in Dayton, Ohio. Military planners at Wright-Patterson Air Force Base's Aeronautical Systems Division began designing a trans-atmospheric vehicle, an airplane that would fly in the air and achieve speeds that would allow it to transfer out of the atmosphere. Within a year, several government agencies joined forces to examine the feasibility of a Mach 25 vehicle, and the concept of an aerospace plane, an airplane that would go from the ground through the atmosphere and then into space, was born. This vehicle, because of its high speeds, required major break-throughs in materials, jet engines, aerodynamics, fuels, and flight controls. Although extremely challenging, it appeared as if these advances might be possible, and the National Aero-Space Plane program was launched in 1985. The program, and its Mach 25 airplane, was a breakthrough in itself. If such a vehicle could be built, its impact on the future could be as great as the impact that the airplane had on the world in 1903. Hypersonic flight in the atmosphere, speeds of 5,000 to 15,000 miles per hour in an air-plane, and an aircraft that could take off and land on conven-tional runways and routinely fly to space would open up many new possibilities. The technology for this aircraft is now being developed, and the feasibility of such an aircraft now seems very real. How that is happening and its relationship to breakthrough leadership is described later in this book.

In 1903, a vision of giant airports filled with hundreds of airplanes that reliably, safely, and affordably take ordinary people across the continent would have been laughable. Today, Mach 25 allows another vision, of giant airports filled with a variety of aircraft that reliably, safely, and affordably take ordinary people around the world or into space. At Mach 25, the sky is not the limit. Mach 25 is breakthrough thinking, and breakthroughs occur when we realize that the sky is not the limit.

Breakthroughs

An aerospace plane, like so many other visions, seems impos-sible in the beginning. We place so many limits on ourselves that most of us believe tomorrow will be pretty much like today or even yesterday. But it isn't, as we can see if we look back over the past year, decade, or century. Change occurs all the time, and these changes affect our lives and the world in very significant ways. There are many people and organizations that don't believe that

today should be like yesterday, and they go about seeking to change the world for the better. These people believe that breakthroughs can occur, that the sky is not necessarily the limit. And they routinely prove that it isn't.

Over the past several decades, we've all lived in a high-tech world. Although certainly not the only place where breakthroughs occur, technological breakthroughs have had an enormous impact on our civilization. Almost everything that affects us today has been significantly altered by a technical breakthrough that occurred not centuries ago but within the past several decades. Look at a day in your life: instant breakfasts; microwave ovens; frozen foods; electric toothbrushes; home air conditioning; garage door openers; high-performance automobiles; reliable, affordable commercial aircraft (supersonic, if you can afford it); personal computers; television; video recorders and players; home exercise machines; fast-food franchises; hot tubs; and, finally, waterbeds. In the past thirty years, there have been thousands of significant breakthroughs in the technical world and many more in the worlds of economics, marketing, law, medicine, etc. Each one represents a major shift in direction and forced a significant change in the world. Although chance, luck, and divine inspiration may have been involved in some aspects of a few of these breakthroughs, they were mostly the result of hard work, human creativity, and a strong drive to achieve the breakthrough. In every case, a barrier, or several of them, was broken in order to attain the end result. Often, this process is referred to as *innovation,* and it is linked to a creative leap in thinking. There's no question that creativity and innovation are part of the breakthrough process. But, contrary to popular thinking, innovation is the end of the process, the reward or outcome of all the activity that precedes the breakthrough. Because innovation represents a leap into the unknown, it's the one part of the process that we can't control very well. The innovative breakthrough seems almost mystical if viewed alone, a spark of genius, which after it is achieved becomes the norm to use for the future. The breakthrough itself cannot be controlled, but much of what's necessary to achieve it can be influenced, stimulated, inspired, encouraged, developed, and fostered. Breakthroughs don't happen by chance; they are the result of organized activity. And because of that, they can be managed. Yes, managed. It seems like a contradiction in terms; managed break-throughs—almost an oxymoron. But that's precisely how they happen.

In order to prove this, we could investigate the history of any famous breakthrough, say the television or the personal computer. To do that, we would have to become very familiar with the real details of the activity which led to the innovation. Unfortunately, no one except the individuals who were directly involved in the activity would be able to give us the real facts behind the event. And even if we could find these people or some recorded history of the breakthrough activity, I'm not sure we would get the true story. Having written and read hundreds of technical papers and disser-tations over the past thirty years, I'm convinced that many events, and, amazingly, some of the most important events in any process, never get recorded. We usually neglect to record the seemingly unimportant failures and mistakes that occur along the way, and some of those misfortunes are often the reason that we went in a particular direction that eventually allowed us to reach our goal. Invariably, the emotions, feelings, and human interactions that are involved in the process are not recorded and rarely recalled or reflected even in conversation. A written translation of the break-through event is usually flawed and may really lead us in the wrong direction in terms of understanding the event.

Fortunately, there is a way of understanding the real story behind these kinds of processes, and it has little to do with other people; we can examine our own breakthrough situations and see what was at work during those events. O.K., so none of us have discovered relativity or invented the video recorder or flown super-sonically for the first time. Those were major league, world-class breakthroughs, and most of us don't get to play at that level. But we all play, even if it's in the minors, at the intramural level, or in little leagues. I'm convinced that each of us has been involved in breakthroughs, some of which may have been very significant. But even if they weren't that big, we have all been involved in a project that resulted in a new way of doing something, or that showed a way to do something differently, or that produced something dif-ferent for the very first time. These breakthrough events happen to all of us, not all of the time, but occasionally. Usually, they are the best times of our lives, at least of our professional, if not our personal, lives. These are the times that we are at our best, and they invariably result in some sort of breakthrough.

Examine what happened during these times. Recall a time in your life when you were involved in a project that resulted in something that made you very proud. Another approach might be to search for a time in your life when you were making a difference or performing at your best. It doesn't matter if this was a personal or professional experience or when in your life it occurred. Some people have many of these experiences while others have several, but everyone seems to have at least one that they can recall. Focus for a moment on the end result of the activity. Did it involve a change or improvement? Was it significant enough to be noticed by others not involved in the project? Did it set a new standard or approach for what came after the project? Did it make a difference? If you can answer yes to any of these questions, you were involved in a breakthrough. Some barrier was broken, and you ended up making a contribution that influenced the way things were.

The Elements of Breakthroughs

Continue with your personal breakthrough experience for a while longer and examine how it happened. As you recall your experience, focus on the situation, the purpose, the strategy, the results, and the character of the experience, and try to answer the following questions:

The Situation

- Where did this take place?

- When did this take place?

- Who was involved?

- What was your personal role?

The Purpose

- Why was the activity done?

- Who motivated the activity?

- What outcome was desired?

- What was the primary goal?

The Strategy

- How was the objective achieved?

- What techniques were used?

- What structures were implemented?

- What actions were taken?

The Results

- What were the actual results?

- What were the measurable outcomes?

- What were the qualitative results?

- What recognition was received?

The Character

- How did you feel during the activity?

- What was the quality of the experience?

- What made the difference?

- How did the team relate?

Now that the details of the experience are fresh in your mind, try to summarize the characteristics or conditions of the experience using a few key words or short phrases. Usually ten or so characteristics are sufficient for most people to capture the essence of the experience, and words and phrases like "clear purpose," "challenging," "exhilarating," etc. are often used. Before you go on, list your key words on the side of this page so that you might compare them with those of the many others who have completed this exercise.

Over the past ten years, I've asked over 20,000 individuals to go through a similar memory and characterization exercise with respect to a breakthrough experience. A very few of these people had world-class breakthroughs; most of them were just ordinary people who initially would never have admitted to being involved in a breakthrough. After thinking about it for a while, however, every one of them could recall an experience that fit into the definition of breakthrough that I've used earlier in this chapter; not a single exception, and the age range was from eighteen to eighty. For many, the breakthrough experience was a singular event in their lives, and they recalled it with great excitement and joy. Others had experienced a few breakthroughs, and they were able to compare the characteristics of one against the other. For a very few, their lives seemed to be one breakthrough after another, and they had difficulty choosing one to probe. After talking at length with these few rare individuals, it became apparent that their entire lives were structured around the very characteristics that are the subject of this book. That is, a large number of breakthroughs occurred in these people's lives because they lived their lives with that very intention. Not surprisingly, some of these individuals were responsible for some rather major breakthroughs, although only a small percentage of their breakthroughs fell into that category.

With 20,000 people each coming up with ten or so characteristics of their individual experience, you might expect to see a pretty long cumulative list (since there are certainly over 200,000 words and phrases in the English language, we could have reached that number). Actually, a total of less than 200 words or phrases have emerged after ten years, and of those, about a dozen clearly stand out as typical of almost every breakthrough experience. Here they are as they are usually stated:

Important Purpose

Clear Goal

Challenge

Team Effort

Freedom

Excitement

Contribution of Everyone Involved

Strong Commitment

Persistence

Fun

Trust

Hard Work

These are the key characteristics that have led to breakthroughs for thousands of individuals. Certainly, they should provide us with some insight into the circumstances that might stimulate breakthroughs under more general conditions. As we weave several of the other words that have come out of the individual experiences with the previous dozen, some patterns emerge. Clearly, *purpose* is an important factor: the more challenging the purpose, the more excitement it generated. Once people get hooked into a challenge that they feel is worthwhile, they are headed towards the needed breakthrough. *Focus* is often discussed as the technique that was used to keep their endeavors on track; otherwise, the energy needed to achieve the end result seemed to dissipate. In almost every case, more than one individual was involved, and *collaboration* is often cited as a key ingredient. Generally, the individual team members had different skills, personalities, and capabilities. Yet, they eventually used the combined talents of the team to pull off the breakthrough and, at least in retrospect, the differences in the team members were appreciated. Most stories have wonderful examples of extraordinary *support* and *trust* given to the team, allowing the needed creativity and risk-taking to occur. Many individuals also told of times of great uncertainty, and even failure, during their experience. During these periods, *commitment* to succeed, to overcome the challenges, and to achieve the goal was the driving force that moved them to the breakthrough. And, finally, there is the spirit of the experience. Only a handful of individuals out of 20,000 did not agree that their experience was both exciting and fun. Often the word "*adventure*" comes up. Many agreed that, in retrospect, their breakthrough experience was one of the great adventures of their lives.

NASP

The National Aero-Space Plane (NASP) program, which was one of the key catalysts for this book, is an interesting case study on breakthroughs. It began because of the conviction of several people that an aerospace plane could be developed by achieving simultaneous breakthroughs in several fields of science and engineering. The challenge for them was to develop the technologies that would allow construction of an airplane which could go far and fast enough to become a spacecraft. Since space launch systems were quite routine in 1985, it wasn't the end point that fascinated these people—it was getting to that point. They were captivated by the idea of an airplane, not a rocket, that would fly at hypersonic speeds and eventually reach Mach 25, the escape velocity for low earth orbital flight. They were also stimulated by what such a plane would represent from a purely aeronautical standpoint. Since no airplane had ever been developed that could fly faster than four times the speed of sound, a Mach 25 airplane was clearly a breakthrough that excited their imagination.

Although the concept of aerospace planes routinely traveling from earth to space (as do subsonic airplanes from airport to airport) set the vision, it was clear to the early NASP pioneers that more focus was required in order to develop the technology needed for such an airplane. While the vision provided the purpose for the team, it was so challenging that almost any type of research and development activity could be justified. The team needed more focus in order to target and direct their activities. Thus the X-30 concept was created—an experimental aircraft that would demonstrate all of the technologies needed to produce an aerospace plane.

Conceptual drawings of the X-30 experimental airplane began to emerge early in the program, and all of the research and development efforts were focused on defining or validating the evolving design of the X-30. Curiously, there were so many unknowns at the beginning of the NASP program that a design for an experimental vehicle that would fly five to ten years later was absolutely premature. Yet, the team chose the X-30 as the cornerstone of the program. Purposely, however, they allowed and encouraged great latitude and flexibility in the preliminary designs of this vehicle. This openness to change allowed them to integrate both the positive and the negative results of the ongoing research and development programs in the evolution of the X-30 design. It also stimulated creativity among the members of the team since nothing was really fixed, and anyone had a chance to make a contribution to the ultimate vision and its manifestation through the X-30 experimental aircraft.

When the program began in 1985, there were less than 200 scientists and engineers in the United States with any background or experience in hypersonic aircraft or hypersonic propulsion. Most of these people were in a few government laboratories that had kept the "hypersonic flame" alive during the 60s and 70s, when such advanced research was not being supported by significant government or industrial funding. It was clear, however, that a few hundred people would not suffice to produce an aerospace plane capability. By 1988, a national team of several thousand people in over 400 government, industrial, and academic organizations was in place. Although several of the larger companies were in direct competition for the eventual X-30 aircraft program, they were bonded to each other by a common goal and the need to collaborate if the required breakthroughs were to occur. From 1988 to 1992, the large national team evolved from a loosely integrated array of competing individual contributors to a national consortium, then to an industrial joint venture partnership, and, finally, to one single government/industry/academic national team, the first of its kind in the United States. The need for collaboration to achieve the breakthroughs overcame the normal division of responsibility between the government and industry and the competitive nature of American industry.

Throughout its brief history, the NASP program has also been a great experiment in the management of aerospace research and development. Generally, most aerospace R&D is conducted by laboratories in government, industry, and academia that do discipline-oriented research and development. The mission of these laboratories is to improve the technology of materials, electronics, propulsion, etc., so that future aircraft and space systems will have greater capabilities or better performance. The activities in these laboratories are driven by technological improvements rather than the specific needs of a future system. Unlike discipline-oriented R&D, the NASP program is very focused on its eventual product, an aerospace plane, and conducts research and development specifically to achieve this goal. Such an effort is generally referred to as focused R&D. In order to produce breakthroughs in a focused R&D program, the R&D must be conducted in very creative and flexible ways, yet it must always be evaluated with respect to its contribution to the focus of the program. This structured flexibility also applies to the organizational and management aspects of the program, which resulted in a blend of "adhocracy" and bureaucracy. Although difficult to implement, it was necessary for a situation like NASP, where the simultaneous achievement of multiple breakthroughs is required, in order to achieve a very challenging objective.

While the NASP program appears to have obvious benefits that would be of great value to the nation, it has been a program plagued by great uncertainty, instability, and questions. During each of its first six years, the program was cancelled by either the administration or Congress. Fortunately, compromises were reached by the end of the annual budget cycle so that funding was authorized and the program was not terminated. Because it is a joint program involving several agencies and receives very high-level attention (the vice president oversees the program), it is a highly political activity. This results in the usual interpersonal and interorganizational rivalries and conflicts. Several key managers, including my predecessor, were fired, and many program participants took on professional risk by being associated with NASP. In addition, the great technical challenges, coupled with the managerial and political uncertainties, have placed unusual pressure on the team over the six-year period. It has only been through great personal commitment that the team has remained bound and determined to develop the technologies needed for an aerospace plane. Despite continuing evidence that abandoning the project would be in their best interest, most of the team has remained true to the vision and are committed to seeing it to completion, regardless of the sacrifices required.

To counter the difficult challenges and political uncertainties, the program leadership has always emphasized the potential impact and payoff of the effort. From the beginning, the effort was open only to volunteers eager to make a difference in the history of aviation and space. From its motto "NASP—The Sky Is No Longer the Limit" to multimedia NASP program presentations that depict the tremendous significance of the vision, the focus has always been on the breakthrough nature of NASP. Usually the vision is so captivating that at most presentations on NASP someone in the audience is stimulated to join the team. The program is both an adventure and a quantum leap into the future. This has generated tremendous excitement and energy both inside and outside the team. It's been this energy that has allowed the team to stay focused on the breakthrough.

Managing for Breakthroughs

Can breakthroughs be made to happen? Can they be managed? If you look at the general characteristics that emerged during the ten-year study and relate those to the NASP program, the answer seems to be yes!

At some point in a breakthrough experience, the individuals on the team seem to get captivated by a challenge. Sometimes it's directed at them from above, and they accept it because of the potential professional or personal gain. Sometimes, it's self-generated because of their desire to do something better, to make a contribution, or perhaps to make a difference. In other cases, it's because they can't go on without a breakthrough. They are blocked, and they need to solve the problem or generate a new solution. The challenge captures their minds, and usually their hearts, and off they go.

Once captivated, the team members set their direction by focusing on something that can be defined. If they want to change the world of personal computers, they begin to focus on a computer that is like a person—friendly, fun, and unique. If they want to fly like a bird, they begin building an airplane that uses human power for propulsion. In almost every case, the focal point changes form during the course of the project, but it remains the focus of the activity. The focus provides the general direction for the team, but some deviation from the original prototype or starting point always seems to occur. This openness to change, improvement, and modification yields the creativity and innovation that are at the core of the breakthrough. Without the freedom to deviate from the path, the initial direction will restrict the solutions, and breakthroughs will not occur. During the course of the endeavor, the team may very well depart from the original concept. The focus, however, provides them with a beacon to steer their activity.

In the complex world of the 20th century, the lone inventor working by himself to achieve a breakthrough is an extremely rare exception, and certainly is not the rule. While specific individuals may get cited for a breakthrough, generally there are co-workers or teams behind the leaders. Often the team itself makes the breakthrough, and it is recognized for the achievement. When the team makeup is analyzed, we often discover that the individuals are very different from each other. While conflicts can and do occur, the differences contribute to the richness of the result. The competition to meet their individual personal and professional needs blends into a collaboration to achieve the required composite solution. If there is no competition within the team, the solution may come quicker, but at the expense of depth and quality. Competition provides the spark that most people need to go the extra length. In a team, it makes the entire team push harder.

The setting for the breakthrough is usually both stimulating and supportive. While some breakthroughs occur in chaotic and disruptive environments, a basic structure that allows persistent, organized activity seems to be enhancing. The required resources

[handwritten marginalia: "like this observations"]

must be available or attainable; otherwise the team will not be able to go on. Personal survival, although sometimes a stimulant, is generally not at stake in most breakthroughs. There is a blend of structure and "unstructure," enough to provide some stability and security, but just enough to do that. Superimposed on that structure is great freedom and flexibility to bend the rules, change the norms, and generate the breakthrough.

like this !! .

More than anything, the key ingredient seems to be commitment. Breakthroughs are usually tough to achieve, and it generally takes great willpower to stay the course. Things will go bad, there will be failures and breakdowns, and obstacles will get in the way. Determination, dedication, and persistence, and, sometimes, extraordinary doses of all three, are often necessary to achieve the goal. While the team can subscribe to being committed, it always ends up at the personal level. At the end of the road, when the breakthrough finally occurs, it's the individual commitment that determines who is left on the team.

Finally, there is the element of adventure, the journey into the unknown, the search for the Holy Grail, the slaying of the dragon, the climb to the top. Perhaps this is the mechanism that links all of the factors required for breakthroughs. In any breakthrough experience, the challenges are difficult, the road is uncertain, sacrifice and diligence are the norms, and confusion and instability plague the team. Evaluated logically, these conditions would suggest abandoning the project. But these are the same circumstances that we encounter in journeying to another land, changing jobs, embarking on a new career, or falling in love. We have all experienced these situations; they are the adventures of our lives. Similarly, the breakthrough experiences are the adventures of our careers.

All of the evidence points to one conclusion: Breakthroughs can be managed. It's primarily a matter of doing what has worked in the past—recreating the conditions that could lead to a breakthrough. Like any technique involving people and organizations, breakthrough management may not always yield the desired result. But our experiences tell us that some, if not most, of the time it will, and that's a breakthrough in itself.

Breakthrough Leadership

To summarize, it seems that breakthroughs occur when:

- Someone or some team really gets captivated with a vision or a challenge.

- A focus for the activity is selected, but that focus is kept open to innovation, creativity, and change.

- The individual or team enlists the aid of others in achieving the breakthrough. The diversity of opinion results in conflict and competition of ideas, but the collaborative effort yields the synergy required for the breakthrough.

- The setting is a blend of flexibility and structure. Neither "adhocracy" nor bureaucracy, the environment provides the opportunity to be creative, to be different, and to take chances.

- Failures, disappointments, and setbacks are overcome by personal and team commitment to see it through. Determination and persistence allow the team to break through the barriers.

- A sense of adventure keeps the spirits high and supports the commitment. Bonding, excitement, and intensity characterize the activity.

Basically, the *characteristics of the breakthrough process* are:

Captivating Challenges

Open Focus

Competitive Collaboration

Structured Flexibility

Personal Commitment

Organized Adventure

If these are the keys to breakthroughs, then the task of break-through leadership is to create these conditions. If the places where breakthroughs occur look like this, then the job of leadership is to lead our teams to these places. The mission of breakthrough leaders, then, is to:

- Develop the challenges that captivate the hearts and minds of our people.

- Keep the team focused but allow and encourage an openness to new approaches.

- Foster and stimulate diverse opinions, collaboration, creativity, and difference in order to achieve synergism.

- Provide a setting and support system that is both structured for stability and flexible enough to allow innovation.

- Personify, in every way, unwavering commitment to the goals in order to stimulate the same behavior in the team.

- Make it an adventure.

Sometimes the leader is a distinct part of the team; that is, the leader's principal job is with a single team. In these cases, the leadership role can range from strong involvement in every aspect of the breakthrough project to one of a boundary manager to assure that the conditions for breakthrough are provided or main-tained. In other instances, a leader may be responsible for the activities of many individuals or teams that have the potential of achieving breakthroughs. In these cases, the leader's job is more complex and must accommodate the multiple activities under his direction. And, of course, there are cases in between and outside of these two classes. Nevertheless, the characteristics for breakthroughs are the same. Hence, there are common behaviors for any leader who is interested in achieving a breakthrough.

While the preceding examples emphasized professional and technical situations, the characteristics and required behavior for breakthroughs should apply to any situation, from developing a hypersonic airplane to changing the shape of your body. After all, wouldn't shedding twenty-five pounds in two months (surely a minor breakthrough for many people) involve the challenge of the task, a vision of a slimmer you, a diet with some flexibility for cheating, a little help from your friends, some real conflict (both inside and out), some significant change in your life without giving up the basics, a tremendous personal commitment, a good attitude, and a great feeling of accomplishment as you succeed? With diets, we're talking about breakthroughs on a personal level, but the principles are the same.

Breakthroughs don't just happen. The conditions are set, and then you hope that the breakthroughs occur. Leaders cannot guarantee that breakthroughs will occur, but they can at least set the conditions so that the odds are much better. In the next six chapters, we'll examine each of the key characteristics of breakthrough leadership and look at how various leaders, managers, and individual contributors have increased the odds and helped their teams achieve the breakthrough.

CHAPTER 2

Captivating Challenges
The Target

To dream the impossible dream,
to fight the unbeatable foe.
To bear the unbearable sorrow,
to run where the brave dare not go.
This is my quest, to follow that star,
no matter how hopeless, no matter how far.
To fight for the right, without question or pause.
To be willing to march into hell
for a heavenly cause.
—The Man of La Mancha

Whether it's in their professional or their personal lives, most people want to make a difference. Given half the chance, many folks would jump at the opportunity to do something that would leave a mark on their organization or community. Fortunately for most of us, our basic needs for food, shelter, employment, and acceptance have been met. What we would really like to do is make a contribution in our sphere of influence. What's more, many of us just love the idea of a challenge. If someone sets the bar one notch higher, we consider it a personal challenge to our capabilities. Dare us, and we respond; block us, and we try to overcome the obstacle; make us an underdog, and we fight even harder.

Our fascination with a challenge and our need to make a difference have resulted in some incredible breakthroughs. Football teams have emerged from devastating defeats and gone on to win championships. Paraplegics have, with the help of their doctors and computerized electronic stimulation, walked down the aisle to receive a diploma or get married. Polio has been conquered and many forms of cancer are being controlled. The Soviet Union has gone from communism to capitalism. The U.S. put a man on the moon ahead of schedule and a world coalition recently fought a major war against Iraq with minimum casualties. All of these events point to one thing—captivating challenges are a key ingredient in producing breakthroughs. If people feel that their mission is challenging and important, they will pursue it with determination and creativity. If the goal is a real stretch, then a breakthrough may be the only way to achieve it. The tougher the challenge, the bigger the breakthrough; the more captivating the challenge, the greater the commitment to achieving the breakthrough. Achieving breakthroughs is a lot like a fascinating journey. If you make the destination challenging and exciting, some people will do incredible things to get there.

The Carroll High School Marching Band

All of my daughters attended the same high school, which is about two miles from where we live. While they are three very different individuals (Karen is an accountant, Kristen is an engineer, and Kim is still studying to be a psychologist), they all became involved with the marching band at Carroll High School. As most "band parents" can attest, if your child is in the band, you are in the band. I've attended more band rehearsals, marching competitions, and fund-raising events than I care to remember. Usually it was a lot of fun, whether they won or lost, played well or not, made money or broke even. For me, there was an added value. I was able to watch the band director and his assistants try to shape this unorganized gang of stumbling, would-be musicians into a precise, regimented, melodious marching band in about three months, every year for ten consecutive years. Developing an aerospace plane is a piece of cake compared to what this guy had to do, and it was fun watching him do it.

Carroll High School has about 1,000 students that come from five parochial elementary schools in the area. It's a fine school, but certainly not the best school in the city with respect to marching bands. The band supports social and sporting events and every so often has a good year when the sound is reasonable and the students don't collide with each other as they march on the field. Up until 1983, its major claims to fame were the spiffy red, white, and blue Patriots outfits worn by the band members and a very vocal and dedicated following of band parents. In 1983, however, several things happened that made a big difference to the Carroll High School Marching Band. Fortunately, I had a ringside seat for these events since my middle daughter, Kristen, was the field commander of the band in 1983.

For one thing, it was to be band director Dave Luzio's last year. He was going on to another position, and he was determined to make his final year count. The band had also retained many of the junior and sophomore players from the year before, so it had a bit more experience than usual. And the fund-raising events of the previous years had filled the coffers with enough cash to re-outfit some of the team with new uniforms. Armed with these capabilities and a now-or-never attitude, Luzio decided to go for broke. While a goal of "city champions" might have been ambitious, an attempt to become the best band in Ohio would have been a real stretch. Luzio ignored all reason and decided to go for the *national* championship. When he broke the news of his mission at the first student/parent band meeting that summer, most of us seasoned band parents found it hard to keep a straight face. But we had to because the kids innocently drank in his words, and it was obvious to us that they believed him. He said it several times that night, and before the meeting ended, the kids really thought that they had a chance to win the national championship.

There were several more meetings that summer, and each one ended with a few more parents believing the dream. By the first competition of the fall, we had all bought into this ridiculous crusade and, in the process, the band had been transformed into one which was at least worthy of serious competition. Instead of the usual marching songs, an extremely difficult set of classical scores was chosen. All new uniforms and props were made or procured, and military drill experts were brought in to orchestrate highly complex marching maneuvers for the performance. The kids were absolutely determined to win the championship, and they began to act like champions. Before each competition, they would proclaim that they were going to be "awesome," and they convinced all of us to shout that word as they marched onto the field. The Cincinnati Bengals may be awesome, but it was hard to think of the Carroll High School Marching Band as awesome. Nevertheless, we began to shout it, and they began to look and sound awfully powerful.

As the months progressed, the band got better and better. The awkward gang of teenagers evolved into a professional drill team that played beautiful music. They were magical, and they believed in their own magic. Even Kristen, the toughest and most cynical member of my family, had no doubts about the outcome. In November of 1983, the band competed for the national championship at the Marching Bands of America Nationals in Johnson City, Tennessee. They played very well and videotapes of the marching maneuvers are still used by the high school as a benchmark for the field performance. To give them a little more edge, Luzio asked Kristen several hours before the finals to add a little comedy to the second number. She rented a costume, changed into and out of it during the ten-minute performance, and brought down the house.

Several hours after they had performed, as the band entered the huge field house to receive the National Championship Trophy, 200 proud parents, all dressed in red, white, and blue, screamed at the top of their lungs, "Awesome...Awesome...Awesome...."

The IHPTET Crusade

Most business travelers will agree that the hours spent on airplanes are not the most exciting of our lives. Generally, they're a good time to catch up on some reading or grab a quick nap. Every once in a while, someone friendly sits next to me, and that can lead to an interesting conversation. That's what happened a while back on a long nonstop flight from Los Angeles to Boston.

It was apparent from the magazines my row-mate was reading that her occupation had something to do with food. About ten minutes into the flight, she told me that she was the executive chef for a large hotel in Massachusetts and that she was returning from her corporate headquarters in Los Angeles. I reciprocated by telling her that I was the manager of a research and development organization which developed jet engines. Since I have some good friends at Westin Hotels, I was interested in her approach to customer service. We talked about that for awhile, and I almost had her convinced to leave her company for Westin when we hit some heavy turbulence. She grabbed the arm rest, and her knuckles got white. Somewhat shakily, she asked if the airplane could take this turbulence. In as calm a voice as I could muster, I said, "No problem. I never worry about the airplane; they're built to be flexible, and they can take much more turbulence than what we're feeling." She relaxed a little and seemed to regain some of her composure. But I just couldn't resist, so I said, "What bothers me are those engines. You know, we develop them and do you realize there are over 10,000 parts in those babies...all built by the lowest bidder." I could see her pupils dilating, so I quickly laughed and told her, "I was just kidding, the engines are even more dependable than the airplane." It was a dirty trick, so I bought her a drink to ease my conscience. We talked some more because now she really was interested in jet engines, particularly their reliability. By the time we landed, my own words made me realize once again how terrific jet engines really are. And here I was, part of a crazy crusade to make them much, much better.

The IHPTET (pronounced ip-tet) program is as close to a crusade as I'll ever get. There are knights in shining armor, dragons, infidels, even a Holy Grail. Just the kind of action to excite the young Turks in the Air Force's Propulsion Laboratory. Officially known as the Integrated High Performance Turbine Engine Technology program, IHPTET is an attempt to achieve a breakthrough in aircraft jet engines. For fifty years, excellent progress has been made in jet engine technology. Current commercial and military engines are highly reliable, very fuel efficient, extremely durable, and really amazing in their ability to lift and maneuver aircraft. Everyone who is involved in jet engine development is very comfortable with the advances that have been made over the past five decades. And that's exactly what bothered those of us that started the crusade. Progress has been absolutely steady since the jet engine was invented. Every year, the engines get a little better. Every year, the engineers would change a few things, and every year, the engine performance would improve slightly. Nice and steady, nice and easy.

We wanted more! We all felt that the past was really beginning to determine the future in the development of jet engines. No one was taking any risks, no one was pushing the limits. We knew that much greater progress could be made, but neither the industry nor the government was inclined to even consider changing the pace. We had pushed the leading engine manufacturers and essentially had been thrown out of their front offices. When we asked Washington for help, they thought we were being foolish and were afraid we would jeopardize the balance that had been set up between the government, the engine manufacturers, and the airplane companies. No one would listen to us, and we were frustrated by our inability to get anyone excited about the progress that could be made. Their standard replies were that "better is the enemy of good enough" and "if it ain't broke, don't fix it."

One evening, a few of the engineers in the Propulsion Laboratory got together in my office, primarily to complain about the situation in the jet engine business. In the course of the discussion, one of them drew a simple figure on the blackboard. It was a plot of jet engine performance versus time. On the bottom of the blackboard, he drew a horizontal time line, starting in 1940 and extending to 2040 in segments of ten years. On the left side, he drew a vertical line that went from zero at the bottom to twenty at the top. The vertical line represented the thrust-to-weight ratio of a jet engine; how much thrust the engine puts out in pounds, divided by how much the engine weighs in pounds. An engine's thrust-to-weight ratio is one of the key measures of its performance. Since the historical data clearly shows that jet engines have moved steadily from a zero thrust-to-weight ratio in 1940 to a projected ratio of ten in 1990, he drew a straight line from the zero (1940) point to the ten (1990) point. He then extended the line to show that at that pace, we would get to a thrust to weight of 20 by 2040. "That's the problem," he said, "that's way too long." "So, how fast could you get there?" someone else asked. "Oh, I don't know, maybe by 2030, possibly 2025." "Could we do it in half the time, by 2015?" another inquired. "Boy, that would be tough." Everyone agreed. "What the heck, let's do it by *2005*," someone shouted. First there was silence. Then everyone stared at him, looked at each other, and started laughing. "Why not, let's go for it," we all said. And that was it—an idea that took shape. Crazy or not, that would be our goal. We all pledged allegiance to the decision, broke up the meeting, and headed for a nearby tavern.

The next day, we launched the "crusade." Four hundred years ago, we would have crafted some flags with "20 by 2005" on them, mounted our trusty steeds, and rode off to the Holy Land. We thought of doing that, but, instead, we prepared some overheads, made some airline reservations, and set up some meetings in Washington, D.C. Our reception in Washington, as well as all over the country, was similar to that encountered by King Arthur and his gang when they rode off to the Middle East. Verbal shots were fired, sarcastic arrows were flung; we were definitely not welcomed. We persisted, they stood firm. We persisted more, they stood more firm. This lasted for about six months. Then someone on their side said, "Well, maybe by 2030." A chink in the armor. More raids, more briefings, and a little more success. Finally, we released our "Excalibur": Dr. Hans J.P. von O'Hain, the inventor of the jet engine. He thought that it might be possible to get to 20 by 2005. They couldn't resist. One by one, they came over and by the end of the year, IHPTET had become a national technology development program, jointly funded for about $100 million by the government and industry, with the goal of achieving a jet engine thrust-to-weight ratio of 20 by the year 2005.

The IHPTET program has now been under way for twelve years. An enormous amount of progress has been made in developing materials, component structures, aerodynamic design, and fuel efficiency since the program began. In 1992, a jet engine was tested which demonstrated a thrust-to-weight ratio of 13. In 1995, we demonstrated an engine with a ratio of 15. Drawing a line through these two new data points indicates that a thrust-to-weight ratio of 20 should be obtained by 2005. Who knows if we'll actually achieve our goal. But if we hadn't set our goal so high, we would never have come so far, so fast. And, since we have, we just might make the goal.

Important message.

Wooden Airplanes

In the fall of 1989, the commander of Wright-Patterson asked several of us from the base to attend a planning meeting for the 1990 Dayton Air Show. While Dayton has sponsored an air show since 1975, the 1990 show was going to be a very special event. The city had been competing with several other air shows held annually in the country for the title of U.S. Air Show, and it looked like Dayton might be able to capture the prize in 1990—providing the air show was spectacular. Turning to its foremost tenant, the city fathers had asked the Air Force base for special assistance this particular year in an attempt to go all out with aircraft displays and flying events. The meeting was the first of several to put the Air Force base solidly behind the 1990 Dayton Air Show endeavor.

The request for my attendance at the meeting left me a little confused. The air show people wanted dozens of airplanes for their static displays: the more, the better; the bigger, the better. If possible, they wanted airplanes that could fly over the show and give the huge crowds some thrills and excitement. While there were many program directors at the base who could satisfy these requests, I was not one of them. NASP is a research and development program; we have lots of experimental apparatus and tons of test reports, but we didn't have an airplane yet. We might have an airplane for Air Show 2000, but we had nothing but some strange-looking materials and engines in 1989. What could we possibly contribute to the upcoming Dayton Air Show?

When it came to my turn, I told the air show organizers that the only airplane I had available to display was a one-foot model that I had on my desk—they were welcome to it. We all agreed that it would not do the trick. If we could only magnify it fifty or sixty times, we might have something. But, of course, that was impossible. The discussion turned to some other subjects, but I couldn't get the idea of a giant version of my desk model out of my mind. Wouldn't it be great to have a huge mock-up of the NASP so that people all over the country could see what the real aerospace plane might look like someday. My reverie lasted until the end of the meeting. When it was just about to end, some demon inside my head made me blurt out the craziest promise I've ever made. I said,

In the left margin, handwritten: My Mom always say if you don't try, you will never get anywhere.

"O.K., we'll have a full-size NASP airplane for the air show; exactly when do you need it?" "Wonderful," they said, "Have it in Dayton by May 1st, and we'll make it the central display at the air show."

As I walked back to my office, my stomach began to churn. There was no way to deliver a full-size NASP in seven-and-a-half months. We might be able to make one out of simple materials, like aluminum and wood, but it would never look like the real thing. And who would do it? Certainly not the government or our industrial contractors. Besides, there was no money to pay for the construction, since our funding could only be used for R&D on the real thing. As usual, I had gotten myself in a fix, and it looked pretty bad. Even worse, I would embarrass the NASP team in front of some very important people and let some good folks down.

When I revealed the situation to my cohorts in the program office, they all agreed that the situation was hopeless. We sat around for a long time wracking our brains for a solution to the dilemma. Somewhere in that process, one of the guys recalled that some university had constructed a paper version of a hypersonic airplane for their homecoming parade. It hadn't been very sturdy or attractive, but maybe we could do something like that. One thing led to another, and we decided that a similar approach was our only hope. The answer was to get some school to build us a giant mock-up of the desk model. The real trick would be to get them to do it for free by May 1st, and it had to look like a real airplane.

Thank God there are dedicated and committed teachers and eager and enthusiastic students still left in this country. Within a week, we found some folks who were willing to give it a try: a group of undergraduate students who had registered for the mechanical engineering design class at Virginia Institute of Technology in Blacksburg, Virginia. One of the engineers in the NASP office had a daughter at Virginia Tech, and, during a visit to the school, he convinced one of the professors to buy into our crazy scheme. Here was the deal: The professor would have the class design an 85-foot airplane using the desk model as a basis. The engineer would serve as our liaison with the professor; he would be able to visit his daughter on weekends and simultaneously monitor the progress of the students. In December, we would look at their design and decide if the kids could actually build the airplane. If they could, we would help them get donations of materials and supplies to construct the mock-up. Late in April, we would send a team of engineers to Blacksburg to inspect the finished product and to see if it met our safety standards and display criteria. If it did, we would provide transportation of the airplane to Dayton for the air show. It was certainly a long shot, but if the students could pull it off, it would satisfy our needs and be a tremendous bargain to boot.

I received a status report on the NASP mock-up project about every three weeks, when the NASP engineer visited his daughter. He kept reporting good progress and was amazed at how hard the students were working. The design was approved in December, and the design class decided to do the fabrication as a senior project. Several more faculty members and a dozen additional students, including some who were not in engineering, joined the team. While the official college status of the project was a four-credit-hour design course, most of the kids were spending twenty to thirty hours a week on the effort. There was no problem finding sponsors and donors for the materials. The enormity of the undertaking fascinated the companies, and they not only contributed materials, but often donated labor and services to the university team. By February, the students had taken over and modified an Aero Club hangar near the university where night and day production shifts worked continuously. The engineer's status reports became more enthusiastic every week. It looked like the kids were going to make the schedule, and it appeared as if the finished product would look reasonably authentic.

Late in February, a senior manager in the National Aeronautics and Space Administration got wind of the project and contacted us with an inquiry. Because of some mess-up, the principal display for the U.S. Pavilion at the Paris Air Show was not going to be available in time for the June event. They had nowhere to turn, and they were interested in looking at the NASP mock-up as a substitute for the now-cancelled display. This was even crazier than my promise to the Dayton people—using the Virginia Tech mock-up as the primary U.S. entry at the prestigious Paris Air Show. At first, we said no, then maybe, but only if the kids agreed. They did in a flash, and the stakes got even higher—delivery in April of an absolutely first-class product.

After that, I almost didn't want to know what was going on in Blacksburg. I could imagine the pressure on these kids and on their professors. I envisioned the entire mechanical engineering department flunking out of all of their other classes because of their commitment to this project. And how in the world were they making ends meet to get the needed supplies and help?

In late March, the lead professor told us that he wanted to deliver the NASP mock-up in a simulated airplane roll-out on April 5th. He assured us that the product was outstanding and that it would be ready on time for both the Paris and U.S. air shows. He convinced us that we should make the roll-out a very big deal and that we should invite some dignitaries from Washington. On April 5th, more than a dozen senior officials from NASA and the Air Force flew into the little airport in Blacksburg, Virginia. Included in the party was the president's science advisor and a representative of the vice president of the United States. There were bands playing, flags flying, thousands of students and parents on hand, and a huge multimedia press corps. After the usual protocol and opening remarks, the doors of the hangar opened and out marched forty students, followed by the most beautiful "almost-an-airplane" that I've ever seen. It was a perfect replica of the desk model, only 85 feet long. The wooden airplane weighed 3,000 pounds and had six layers of fiberglass and an absolutely beautiful paint job. It was so realistic that it was difficult for all of us to believe that this was not the real NASP. At that moment, I thought that it really didn't matter if I ever saw the real NASP because this mock-up was close enough.

After the roll-out event, we transported the NASP mock-up to a nearby Air Force base, flew in a huge C-5A transport vehicle, loaded the mock-up in its belly, and flew it to Paris. Many of the students were allowed to accompany the mock-up to the Paris Air Show, where it was mounted on a giant pedestal outside of the U.S. Pavilion. It became the highlight of the Paris Air Show, and we soon began seeing pictures of our mock-up, surrounded by the kids, in the international trade papers. After Paris, the NASP mock-up was flown back to Dayton, along with the students, where it again became the premier display at the first-ever U.S. Air Show. Fortunately, all of the students graduated that summer and not

We could create something big as long as we have a strong commitment into the project.

one of them ever complained about the long hours spent on the project. Some of them are now working on the NASP program, making important contributions toward the achievement of a real, not wooden, NASP airplane.

Two years later, over a glass of vodka in a quiet restaurant in Washington, D.C., the head of the Soviet Institute of Aeronautics and Gasdynamics winked at me as he politely called me a liar. "My friend," he said, "you cannot fool us about your progress on the NASP program. You see, we know that you built the craft two years ago and that you are much further along than you claim. You cannot hide from our satellites. But, at least tell me this. Why on earth did you construct it in a makeshift hangar on a tiny airfield in a remote part of Virginia?"

Copper Canyon

When the National Aero-Space Plane program first began, it was classified as a secret, limited-access defense program and labeled Copper Canyon. It's not unusual for programs that may lead to a unique military capability to begin or even stay as a limited access project. An aerospace plane certainly could lead to very important defense missions. However, my intuition tells me that there was a second, perhaps equally important, reason for the limited-access label—it added a lot of intangible value to the program. Black programs (as limited-access programs are frequently called) take on an aura of their own. If they are important enough to be black, they must be important enough to work on. And if they are that much of a secret, they become very intriguing and hard to resist. Maybe my gut feeling is wrong, and maybe the second reason never entered anyone's mind. Since I wasn't part of the project in those days, I'll never really know. But there is one thing I do know—the label sure got my attention. It captivated me long before I knew the details of the program. When I was offered the director's job, the fact that it was a black program was not insignificant in my decision to accept the job.

The NASP program was one gigantic captivating challenge from the very beginning. Even today, almost all of the thousands of people involved in the program are still sold on the vision and the contribution that they can make to the vision. The project that comes closest to NASP in intensity and vision is the Apollo program that led to the moon landing in 1969. Like Apollo, NASP is a space program of large proportions, but it also embodies the features of an ultimate airplane, which broadens its appeal to the aerospace world. From the very beginning, that's how the originators wanted it to be.

It all started as the brainchild of a few aerospace zealots who were connected through government and industry friendships. In 1985, Bob Williams from the Defense Advanced Research Projects Agency (DARPA) and his industrial compatriot Tony duPont from duPont Aerospace began looking into the feasibility of designing an airplane that could fly to Mach 25, the speed needed to orbit the earth. While the concept of an aerospace plane had been investigated and subsequently discarded in the 60s, Williams and duPont felt that the advances made in materials, propulsion, and computational analyses in the 60s, 70s, and 80s might change the answer. As duPont analyzed the airplane, Williams got more excited and interested in pursuing a program to develop such an aircraft. After months of analyses, the two concluded that it was feasible to design an aerospace plane and that such a plane could be built provided a tremendous amount of research and development was conducted on the various subcomponents of the plane. In retrospect, the design that Williams and duPont came up with was not a feasible system, nor was it possible to develop the required technology in anything like the ten years that had been estimated. Nevertheless, the NASP airplane, which, in 1985, was estimated to weight only 50,000 pounds fully fueled, was the most exciting aircraft ever designed. Although it required major advances in every significant aerospace technology, NASP promised two of the most exciting breakthroughs since the discovery of the airplane—transportation to space which was so routine and affordable that it was comparable to commercial passenger flights between cities and aircraft that could fly to and from any place in the world in less than two hours. What a package!

The aerospace plane concept mesmerized almost everyone that Williams and duPont briefed. Knowing that he would need the support of many agencies and influential people to acquire resources for the program, Williams used both the vision and the challenge to win supporters. Over a six-month period, he enlisted the help of General Larry Skantze, then Commander of the Air Force Systems Command (he was fascinated with the military potential); former X-15 test pilot and then congressional staffer Scott Crossfield (he saw it as the ultimate experimental aircraft); Dr. Fred Billig, pioneer researcher in scramjet propulsion systems (his engines would be needed to power the NASP); Dr. Ray Colladay, then NASA Associate Administrator for Aerospace Science & Technology (he was captured by its high-tech space transportation features); and several other key aerospace leaders. NASP was not only the ultimate technical challenge, it offered something worthwhile to all of the players. The R&D communities of the Air Force, Navy, and NASA would be put to the test, and they loved it. Washington would have a vision that was as exciting as Apollo, and the politicians loved it. And the military-industrial-aerospace complex would have a new vehicle, and they loved it. Williams even got to President Reagan, and when he heard that it might be able to go from Washington, D.C. to Tokyo in one hour, he loved it. He included the description of the program in his 1986 State-of-the-Union address and referred to it as the Orient Express, a label that we have been trying to remove since.

Beginning with two people in 1985, the NASP program gained supporters by the dozens. By 1987, over 1,000 people were involved in the program, industry was contributing over $100 million of their own R&D money to the effort, the five-agency government sponsoring group was delivering $150 million/year in funding, and people were leaving their comfortable government and industrial jobs (as I did) just to be part of the program. It was a masterful exercise in leadership by Williams and duPont, both visionaries and catalysts. While their calculations and results were optimistic, they believed in the potential of the program, and they used both the possibilities and the challenges to capture the NASP team. While all of the potential has not materialized, and some of the challenges have not been met, the team has successfully maintained the momentum of the program and has delivered an array of breakthroughs in technology, design, computation, and management in order to make the dream come true. To this day, almost everyone ever touched by the program is still captivated by

※ VISIONER

the vision of an aerospace plane and the challenges that it offers. And that challenge continues to motivate them to come up with the breakthroughs necessary to make the vision happen.

Principles

There are times in each of our lives when we have accomplished really incredible things. If we dissect these situations, a single element is generally at the bottom of these accomplishments—the goal or mission of the endeavor had to be worthy of our greatest efforts. Maybe it was winning a championship, landing an important job, creating a successful business, or capturing the heart of our first love. If it was important enough to us, then no effort was too great to assure success. We wanted to succeed badly enough that we were willing to do almost anything to make it happen. The goal was challenging, and we were motivated to meet the challenge. Had it not been challenging, then just a little work would have gotten us there. Had we not been motivated, then we never would have surmounted the obstacles that were between us and the goal. Once we are motivated and captivated by the challenge of the goal, then one of the greatest forces in our human arsenal gets activated—determination.

There is almost nothing that can stand in the way of a really determined individual. If mountains can be scaled and oceans can be crossed by people who really want to get to the other side, then simpler things like government bureaucracies, technological challenges, physical limitations, and schedule delays can also be surmounted. If you want it badly enough, you'll find a way of getting it. That's what creativity is all about—finding a way to get around the barrier between you and your goal. Of course, there will be barriers. If there weren't, it wouldn't be a challenge. But motivated people will discover a way around the barriers. They will go over, under, around, and through the barriers to get to the goal. They will find a way to break through whatever is in their way. In doing so, they will create a solution to a problem that appears unsolvable. They will find a new path, they will develop a lateral approach, or they will show us a novel way of operating. The unmotivated individual will look at the circumstances and conclude that the goal cannot be achieved. The captivated person will persist until the circumstances can be changed so that the goal can be achieved.

There is a little card on my desk with two sayings that speak to this issue. One states that no place is too distant for the person who really wants to get there. Next to it is the now famous photograph of the Stars and Stripes planted on the moon's surface. The second is perhaps the most basic definition of a leader: a person who takes us to places that we've never been before. Next to it is a picture of John F. Kennedy. Great leaders do take us to those distant places that we always wanted to go, but never thought that we could get to. Great leaders give us the challenging goals that motivate us to do whatever it takes to get there. Great leaders inspire us to levels of determination that allow us to break through the barriers that stand in our way.

Nothing ever built arose to touch the skies unless someone dreamed that it should. Someone believed that it could and someone willed that it must."

—Charles Kettering

CHAPTER 3

Open Focus
The Flight

All in the golden afternoon,
Full leisurely we glide...
The dream-child moving through a land,
Of wonders wild and new...
Thus grew the tale of Wonderland,
Thus slowly, one by one,
Its quaint events were hammered out,
And now the tale is done,
And home we steer, a merry crew,
Beneath the setting sun.

—Alice in Wonderland

In reviewing our lives, most of us find that we were able to achieve quite a few of the things that we really wanted. That's not to say that we achieved everything that we wanted, but if we really went after something, we usually succeeded. And we were most successful in those areas that were the most important to us. By concentrating our attention and energy in a particular direction, we can really increase our probability of success. If we focus our personal or professional lives on one thing, we may not achieve the ultimate, but we will certainly make a great deal of progress.

I like this

Approaching something helter-skelter is never very productive; it's concentration that gets results. Soft sunlight is warm and pleasant, but if you want to get a fire going, focus the rays with a lens.

Like other achievements, breakthroughs happen when people focus their attention on the issue. While most teams concentrate on the solution, breakthrough teams focus on the challenge and are open to whatever solution meets the test. If the solution is known and well-defined, the team is not likely to arrive at a creative or novel result. By allowing, and even encouraging, departures from the norm, interesting possibilities can and do occur. It's that combination of focus and openness, convergence and divergence, that is the basis for innovation. Jazz, one of the most creative forms of music, is all about departures from a central theme. The first forward pass in football, Einstein's resolution of the discrepancies in physics using relativity, the application of substandard glue to create the post-it-note, the Constitution of the United States—these were all innovations driven by both a strong purpose and the willingness to try something new to achieve that purpose.

This seemingly contradictory term—open focus—is at the heart of all breakthroughs. While breakthroughs require that challenge, commitment, and passion be intensified, focus, while absolutely necessary, needs to be occasionally diffused in order to generate new ideas. Like the seagull flying over the shore, the breakthrough team needs to have one eye on the goal and one eye searching for opportunities. Getting to the destination is very important, but how you get there is even more important. The challenge to the team and its leaders is to maintain this balance of in and out, closing and opening, gliding and thrusting—until the breakthrough is achieved.

The Laser Airplane

It was 3 P.M. on Friday, March 26, 1972, when I got the word to attend the after-hours meeting in the director's office. At the time, I was just finishing up the weekly status report on the space solar power technology program that I managed, and I was feeling pretty good about the job that I had held for two years. It had been a struggle to become accepted in a technical field in which I had little background, but I was now a part of the national solar power "mafia." It was also my first real management position, and I was finally becoming comfortable with managing the twenty scientists and engineers in my group. You get to know people in two years, and I knew these guys, what they could do, what turned them on, and what turned them off.

At 5 P.M., I walked into the director's office and found a place among the group that had gathered. Besides the director and the chief scientist, there were eight of us. With only 300 people in the Propulsion Laboratory, the odds were reasonable that I would have known the other seven guys pretty well, but I didn't. They all came from different divisions of the laboratory, and I had never really worked with any of them in my eight years in the organization. I did know, however, that one of them was always being referred to as Crazy Dave and that another had earned the title of Weird Allen. Crazy Dave got his tag because of his fascination with rocket engine development and the intensity with which he pursued this vocation. It wasn't enough for Dave to work on rockets all day in the laboratory; he brought them home at night. His garage contained several makeshift rockets, and his neighbors were petrified that he would blow himself up, and possibly them with him. Fortunately, Dave was a great engineer, and he still was in one piece in March of 1972.

Weird Allen was an altogether different story. In any organization, there are individuals who march to the beat of different drummers. We all know people like this and usually their expert contributions make up for their contrary behavior. Allen not only heard different drums, but he was in a different band in a different parade. He thought about only two things: caves and lasers. His life mission was to explore all of the caves of the United States, and Dayton provided him with a staging area for excursions into the dark and wet caverns of Kentucky and Ohio. Losing Allen for days or weeks was not unusual. After satisfying his spelunking passions in some deep, black hole, he would surface, take a shower, and show up in the sunlight to do more engineering. And the engineering had to be on lasers. He, like Crazy Dave, made no distinction between day or night, work or play, when it came to engineering.

Unlike Dave's rockets, however, lasers were small and relatively simple, and the rumor was that Allen had dozens of them in his apartment.

In 1972, lasers were just coming onto the scientific scene, and the only lasers generally available were the so-called pulse lasers. These lasers operated with flashing lamps and converted the light into powerful pulses of laser energy. To an observer, the short spurts of colored light coming from the laser rods looked magical, but to Allen, they were almost spiritual. The gossip in the laboratory was that Allen slept with his lasers and that one night they almost did him in. Evidently, he had been working on a laser experiment until very early in the morning. Exhausted, he fell asleep at his workbench, and his arm swung through the laser beam. Several pulses of the laser hit his arm and burned holes into the flesh. While the wounds were not fatal, blood gushed from the punctures, and Allen had to wrap his arm in a towel and get himself to a hospital. In the laboratory the next day, his friends inquired about his bandaged arm. All Allen would say was that he was fine and that the experiment had been a success. It seems that the first thing he did after the accident, even before he stopped the bleeding, was to measure the distance between the holes in his arm so that he could determine the frequency of the laser. Whether the gossip was exaggerated is irrelevant; Allen was just the kind of guy to have done such a thing.

While I didn't know anything about the other five guys, I was beginning to wonder why we had all been assembled and, in particular, why I was included in this strange group. The director put an end to my anxiety when he declared that we all had been chosen for a very special assignment, and from that moment on, we would report directly to him and the chief scientist. Our task was to work with our sister laboratory in Albuquerque to develop a prototype laser weapon and to integrate it into a military airplane. The Weapons Laboratory in New Mexico had the lead on advanced weapon systems, so they would handle the laser part of the project. Our laboratory had the responsibility for integration of engines and power systems into airplanes, so that would be our job. The program had a very high national priority and the director felt that a special task force was needed to pull this off. He had handpicked the eight of us and felt that, together, we had the capability to tackle the challenge. And that was it. He thanked us in advance and said we were to report back to him at 7 A.M. on Monday. As we left his office, he grabbed me by the arm and said, "Oh, by the way, Bart, I'd like you to manage the team."

My weekend was a disaster thinking about Weird Allen, Crazy Dave, and heaven only knows what those other five guys did in their garages at night. A high national priority project to put a laser weapon in an airplane? What does that have to do with solar power in space or even nuclear engineering? My nice, comfy job was gone in a heartbeat. Instead, I was going to be sequestered in the back of the laboratory with these apparent nerds, and my job was to "manage" them.

After four weeks into the project, two things were clear. They were even more weird than I first thought, and all of my attempts to manage them failed. I couldn't even get them to talk to each other! They were all individualists, specialists, loners, and, yes, strange. (It reminded me of my days as an undergraduate at MIT.) Each decided to attack the problem by himself, and we were getting absolutely nowhere fast. Every week, I would report back to the director and the chief scientist that we were becoming familiar with our task and that we would soon be showing some progress. I was lying, of course; I didn't have a clue as to what to do, and I had resolved that I would come clean at the review meeting scheduled for the next morning. Just before 5 P.M., (Crazy) Dave announced that he had an idea. He asked that we all meet him in the parking lot around 7 P.M. and that we come prepared to work all night if necessary. Since he refused to elaborate, we were intrigued, and we all agreed to show up.

At exactly 7 P.M., Dave drove his old Studebaker into the parking lot. It was a familiar automobile to the group, but tonight it took on a distinct character. Dave had gone home that afternoon and cut a three-foot-diameter hole in the roof of the car with a metal cutter. Without explanation, he asked us all to get in. I ended up in the middle of the front seat, directly under the hole. He handed me a tape recorder and microphone and told me to be ready to record when directed. At that moment, it never occurred to me that I was being managed.

So, off we went into the crisp night; I could see the stars through the hole. We traveled to the other side of the base and finally came to the end of a long road that paralleled the main runway at Wright-Patterson Air Force Base. Dave revved up the engine and lurched the modified Studebaker forward. We accelerated fast, and at sixty miles per hour, Dave told me to turn on the recorder and stick the mike in the hole. It finally dawned on us what Dave was doing. If we were going to put a laser in an airplane, we would have to cut a hole in the plane to allow the beam to escape. Holes in airplanes are bad news; they create tremendous drag and cause terrible havoc inside the aircraft. The dark side of our minds could even envision people being sucked out of the aircraft. Dave had created an automobile simulation of the eventual laser aircraft. By driving at high speeds on the ground and measuring the sound of the air rushing over the hole, we would begin to understand the air flow phenomena and learn how to integrate the laser in the airplane. It was brilliant and the hole in the roof was typical Dave.

There was only one problem. The road was old, narrow, and bumpy. Dave couldn't get the car to go over seventy miles per hour without losing control, and he was determined to make it to 100. We slowed down abruptly, made a U-turn, and headed back up the road to the runway. After a few minutes, we were on the giant runway, and Dave was all smiles. Off we went, full speed ahead, down a runway that was routinely used to land Strategic Air Command bombers carrying nuclear weapons. Knowing that this was unauthorized, Dave turned out the car lights, which made the ride even more exciting. As we hit 100 miles per hour, the Studebaker felt like it would explode. At that point, I was certain we would all die from any one of three causes: the car would crash, a plane would land on us, or we would be shot by a military firing squad. Amazingly, the result was none of the above. Dave got the data that he wanted on the first run, and we returned to our office, unharmed and unnoticed. We spent all night analyzing our data, and, for the first time, the guys became a team. Ideas flowed like jet fuel, and everyone was excited. By dawn, two things were clear: this strange gang of individualists could work like a real team, and, if we didn't kill ourselves, we would probably succeed in our project.

At 8 A.M., we marched into the director's office, tired but proud. The airflow data was clearly a breakthrough, and the chief scientist was very excited. Unfortunately, the director asked how it was obtained, and we decided to come clean. What followed certainly was a moment of truth. If he had wanted, we could have all been fired not just from the project, but probably from the Air Force. He was upset and angry, but he gave us a break. "One more stunt like that, and I'll kill all of you." We got out of his office as quickly as we could, before he changed his mind. Most of us went home to catch some sleep, but one of the guys went off with Dave to help him weld the top back on the Studebaker. Ten years later, Dave was still driving that car.

Sometimes, letting others plan (experiment) do not take away

From that night on, we were a high-performing team. More experiments were developed in order to understand how to modify aircraft to accommodate lasers, and there was a creative buzz within the group. My job was to act as a boundary manager for the team; keeping them satisfied, interfacing with other organizations and the director, and making sure that we didn't do things that were too outrageous. Occasionally, I would find a dynamite cap in a desk or have to extinguish a minor fire, but the team did become a little more reasonable while still maintaining their creative spirit.

my role as manager

Except, of course, for Allen. About six weeks into the project, we lost Allen. Nobody worried very much for about two weeks. We all figured that he was in a cave someplace and that he would surface when he was good and ready. But after a month, we decided that we should look for him. We searched and made some calls, but we couldn't find him. Just about the time that we were going to involve the authorities, he wandered into the office, just as if he had walked back from a coffee break. He asked us all to follow him to a nearby building, and as we entered a four-story-high bay, Allen flipped on the overhead lights. It took about fifteen seconds for the sodium-vapor lamps to reach their full illumination; only then could we fully appreciate what the building contained.

It turned out that Allen had never left the base during the month that we thought he was lost. He and several of his former pals had spent the whole time in the high bay constructing a giant laser. It was so big that it took the entire building to house it, and,

He had not only the tools but also the courage to do it.

unknown to all of us at the time, it was the world's largest electrically activated gas laser. Allen and his friends had scrounged various pipes and parts from around the base to build the device. They also had convinced the local utility service that they needed a little electricity, about a megawatt, wired into the building. The laser itself was made of see-through plastic and had twenty small mirrors that had to be adjusted by hand. Allen had attached foot straps to the top of the laser cavity so that he could stand on it to adjust the mirrors. He also used the color of the gas to determine the right conditions for lasing, so he needed to dim the lights in the building during a laser experiment. The laser beam that would be generated by the electricity was in the high infrared frequency range and was, therefore, invisible to the human eye. Since it was extremely dangerous (a hit from this one would be fatal), Allen had devised a novel way to follow the path of the laser beam as it left his device. He filled the building with balloons; as the laser beam hit the balloons, they would burst, and he could track the beam path.

In a flash, Allen jumped on the laser cavity, dimmed the lights, and started adjusting the mirrors. The rest of us stood there with our mouths open. It was like a Twilight Zone circus act: Allen, straddling the world's largest laser; the purple gas flowing between his legs; a million watts of electricity crackling in the air; a strange darkness throughout the building; and hundreds of balloons floating in the air. Allen pushed the switch, and, sure enough, balloons burst, and the laser beam almost cut a hole through a two-inch steel plate that, fortunately, intercepted its path. Fortunately, because Allen had managed to aim the beam straight at the director's office, and the steel plate was the only thing that stopped it.

To Allen, the laser was a dream come true. He had achieved a breakthrough, the world's largest electrical gas laser constructed from spare parts (and balloons). To the team, the laser represented a unique capability to understand the interaction of high-power lasers with the air surrounding airplanes and the materials at which the lasers were targeted. We still use it today to understand laser interactions with materials. But to the director and the chief scientist, Allen's laser was much more than an engineering demonstration; it was a wonderful way to showcase the project's accomplishments.

At first, we would bring people through and just show them the laser. Then, we began demonstrating its operation and drilling holes in pieces of steel. We became so good at this that we started mounting the damaged steel plates on wood bases and handing them out as souvenirs. As our fame grew, so did the numbers and the rank of the visitors. One day, the undersecretary of defense decided to visit the laser. My job was to explain the demonstration as I walked him to the fourth-floor landing where he could get a good view of the laser operation. For safety reasons, we left his entourage outside and bolted the door to prevent any outsider from coming in. As I walked him up the four flights of metal stairs, I could see that everything was set for the demonstration. Allen was straddling the laser, the lights were dim, and the gas was purple. The balloons were bouncing all over the floor; they seemed bigger than usual, but sometimes that would happen. As we got within two steps from the top, Allen independently decided the conditions were just right and popped the power switch. The laser beam hit the first balloon and every balloon in the place instantaneously exploded. The blast shook the building and almost blew me and the undersecretary off the steps. Fortunately, I grabbed him, and we were able to keep our footing. Outside, the noise and vibration from the blast brought an immediate response from the entourage. They started breaking down the door for fear that the undersecretary had been killed. Everyone was petrified except for Allen. He just looked up and flashed a great big smile. Later, he would admit that he had filled a few of the balloons with acetylene gas in order to make the laser demonstration a little more spectacular for our honored guest. Fortunately, the undersecretary never was told of this slight modification. In fact, the five seconds that followed the blast may have been momentous for the future of laser weapons in the Air Force. As he recovered his footing, he looked at me, his face pale and his eyes glaring, and said, "My God, these lasers are going to make one helluva weapon." And, with the straightest face that I could muster, I agreed.

Within four months from our formation, we had successfully designed an airplane with a hole in it to carry a laser weapon. The airplane was later built and was used for over a decade to investigate the advanced weapon systems that formed the basis for the Strategic Defense Initiative (Star Wars) program. That airplane, called the Advanced Laser Laboratory, has now been retired and sits in front of the Air Force Museum in Dayton, Ohio. When I drive to work in the morning, I pass both the airplane and the old laser building. They bring back great memories of a bunch of crazy guys who somehow pulled off something pretty terrific. I still don't know exactly how it happened, but we accomplished our goal with amazing speed and efficiency. While everyone did their thing, together we got the job done. Individual initiative, team accomplishment, and open focus.

Kim's Anniversary Present

When our youngest daughter, Kim, was twelve years old, she decided that it would be nice to give Marge and me a special anniversary present. Since she had very little money, Kim pondered for weeks about what she could do and finally settled on an elegant, romantic, candlelight dinner. In order to keep the cost down, she enlisted the aid of a friend and decided to prepare and serve the dinner in our home after my wife got off work on the anniversary day. When she announced her intended gift to the both of us, we were surprised and scared. While we love her dearly, Kim was the kid who held the world record for spilling glasses of milk at family meals. Despite desperate attempts on our part to change her behavior, Kim seemed to sustain herself since the age of ten on three items: cereal, Twinkies, and pop. We never worried about her burning herself because she felt that the best use of the top of the kitchen stove was as a counter, and she thought the microwave oven was a breadbox. As for organizing and executing a dinner, her past performance was not very reassuring. Once she almost flooded the house, and her other attempt required the use of a fire extinguisher. Her accomplice offered little basis for hope either. For the past year, they were in the habit of giggling for three straight hours, and every once in a while, they would go into some sort of strange heavy-metal rock frenzy. I would gladly have offered to take all four of us to the nearby steakhouse, figuring that it would be cheaper than the inevitable cleaning of the Kool-Aid out of the carpet.

But Kim had made up her mind, and she would not be deterred. After great attempts to logically dissuade her, we gave up and threw caution to the winds. Since the details of the event were to be a surprise, she also extracted a promise from us to give her great freedom in the implementation of the anniversary dinner. The only deal that we made with her was that all incidental expenses, like emergency room medical care and insurance deductibles, were to come out of her next month's or year's allowance.

During the following several weeks, Kim and her friend seemed to spend all of their waking hours planning the dinner. Never had I seen such commitment, energy, and focus out of my youngest daughter. They strategized, went shopping every day after school, stored the supplies in an "off-limits to parents" chest in her bedroom, and asked for a three-week advance on her allowance. There was lots of giggling and hours on the telephone, but at least they weren't thinking about boys while all this was going on.

On the fateful night, they greeted us at the door in matching cocktail waitress outfits that they had made for the occasion. They looked terrific, perhaps a little too good since they had based the design of their outfits on those worn by the Playboy Bunnies. (Could this be our little girl?) We were led downstairs into the semi-darkened family room and seated at the linen-covered card table complete with formal dinnerware, real silverware (borrowed), and lighted candles. One of them switched on a portable tape player; instead of hard rock, out came Frank Sinatra. Later they told us that they had recorded several hours of mellow music over one of their favorite punk rock cassette tapes. Martinis were served (how did they know how to make them?), followed by a bucket of iced champagne (how did they manage to buy this?). The meal was exquisite, from the glazed strawberries through the homemade lasagne, which they had prepared from scratch. They ended it with a heart-shaped cake with our names outlined in candles and made with our favorite cake mix and frosting. We've never received better service in any restaurant; not a drop of anything was spilled, and I never heard one giggle. We left them each a five-dollar tip and asked if they could do this every weekend.

By any dining standard, the anniversary dinner was not a breakthrough. But for Kim, it was a breakthrough! She wanted it to be an elegant, romantic event, and, sure enough, it was. Because of the circumstances, she was on her own; free to succeed, to do it her way, or to screw it up. But she and her friend pulled it off with flying colors. Had I persisted based on my earlier fears and apprehensions, I would have forced her into lowering her objectives, most likely defocusing her commitment. Surely, I would have restrained her activities and, thereby, her creativity. There were two breakthroughs that evening; one for Kim and her friend, the other for my wife and me. The kids found out what they could do if they had some focus and some freedom. And so did we.

Magic

These days, there's plenty of magic in professional basketball—there's Magic Johnson, the Orlando Magic, and those unbelievable shots that happen almost every game, as if by magic. One of the greatest players in the history of basketball, Bill Russell of the Boston Celtics, speaks of another kind of magic in his book *Second Wind*. Here's what he says:

> Every so often, a Celtic game would heat up so that it would become more than a physical or even mental game, and would be magical. That feeling is difficult to describe, and I certainly never talked about it when I was playing. When it happened, I could feel my play rise to a new level. It came rarely, and would last anywhere from five minutes to a whole quarter or more. Three or four plays were not enough to get it going. It would surround not only me and the other Celtics, but also the players on the other team, and even the referees.

> At that special level, all sorts of odd things happened. The game would be in a white heat of competition, and yet somehow I wouldn't feel competitive—which is a miracle in itself. I'd be putting out the maximum effort, straining, coughing up parts of my lungs as we ran, and yet I never felt the pain. The game would move so quickly that every fake, cut and pass would be surprising, and yet nothing could surprise me. It was almost as if we were playing in slow motion. During those spells, I could almost sense how the next play would develop and where the next shot would be taken. Even before the other team brought the ball in bounds, I could feel it so

keenly that I'd want to shout to my teammates, "It's coming there"—except that I knew everything would change if I did. My premonitions would be consistently correct, and I always felt then that I not only knew all the Celtics by heart, but also all the opposing players, and that they all knew me. There have been many times in my career when I felt moved or joyful, but these were the moments when I had chills pulsing up and down my spine.

Sometimes the feeling would last all the way to the end of the game, and when that happened, I never cared who won. I can honestly say that those few times were the only ones when I did not care. I don't mean that I was a good sport about it— that I'd played my best and had nothing to be ashamed of. On the five or ten occasions when the game ended at that special level, I literally did not care who had won. If we lost, I'd still be as free and high as a sky hawk.

While Russell doesn't use the term open focus, his magic is just that. There have been times in my own life when the same feelings that Bill Russell describes happened to me. When I've tried to analyze these curious periods, they have always been related to very intense situations and a strange capability on my part to view them from a very different perspective. Usually, they occur when I'm extremely preoccupied or anxious about a particular problem or opportunity. After hours, days, or months of concentration, I give in to letting go. My mind wanders from the focus of my attention, and I open myself up to other inputs. Yet, the objective or goal is still present in my mind. Sometimes it takes a long time to get into this transcendental state, because my rational thinking wants me to work on the solution. But I'm better off if I can let go, because new ideas, and even breakthroughs, come to me during these periods.

In some ways, the "magic" of open focus is that it is fundamental to all creativity, because it allows us to look at old things in totally new ways. Almost everyone has experienced similar situations. Take, for instance, the midnight breakthroughs that occur when you awaken in the middle of the night with a solution to a problem that has mystified you for months. Many flashes of genius have been attributed to daydreams and nightmares. Robert Louis

Stevenson would program his mind for creativity by letting himself fall asleep while thinking about a problem or a deadline. By holding a steel ball in his hand, he would assure himself of waking up when his hand relaxed and the released ball would hit the floor. He claimed that just that amount of relaxed concentration gave him his best stories. With others, meditating, fantasizing, relaxing, or diverting their thoughts while putting the real objective in the back of their minds does the trick.

Whether it's intuitive or deliberate, this freedom with focus seems almost magical. And what's more magic than a breakthrough?

The X-30

When the United States began to pursue the development of an airplane that would go from a runway to space and fly at speeds of Mach 25, it had very little evidence that such a concept was realistic. None of the technologies required for the airplane existed, there was no design for the airplane, no industrial infrastructure was available to build the aircraft, and the government proponents who stimulated the activity were neither organized nor funded to pursue the project. The NASP was basically a half-baked concept being pushed as a possibility for the future. In order to be able to discuss this possibility, the NASP team needed something to show to people, some kind of picture that would allow people to decide whether or not they wanted to be a part of the program. Technologists needed to understand what technologies to pursue and how far the state of the art had to be moved in order to allow the airplane to be built. Engineers needed to have some idea of what this plane would look like in order to determine the uses, operations, and complexity of hypersonic aerospace planes. Industries needed to understand the requirements, challenges, and return-on-investment of such a project so that they could decide whether to invest their people and capital in the activity. And the government needed a definition of the concept so that it could plan, organize, direct, and resource the program as a national endeavor. The X-30 satisfied all of these needs and then some.

Almost literally, the X-30 came out of the blue. Faced with the dilemma of not being able to communicate with their would-be supporters, the proponents of the NASP program decided to paint a picture of an aerospace plane. On a light blue background which represented the sky, a very sleek, sexy-looking airplane was drawn in outline form. Since none of the detailed characteristics of an aerospace plane were known, only the simplest features could be defined. The aircraft was long and thin, as you might expect of something that would go Mach 25. It was a cross between a rocket ship and a winged aircraft, with a cylindrical body and small wings for control. Cleverly, a top view of the plane was drawn. Since the engines are on the underside of the body, they could not be seen, and, therefore, they did not have to be drawn. The final touch was to add color, so the plane was portrayed in red, white, and blue, the obvious colors of a national program. Most people never realize that such an airplane would never be painted since much of the paint would burn off long before the plane reached its ultimate hypersonic speeds. The last task was to give the aircraft a name, some kind of designation that would clearly identify it. Because it was only an artist's concept, it certainly could not be the real aerospace plane. Since time and technology would likely force changes in this concept, it had to embody flexibility. So the perfect name was chosen—the X-30—representing the next experimental aircraft in this country's history. The program now had shape, it now had substance (at least a little), and, because there was a picture on a sheet of paper, it now had focus. By declaration, the focus of the NASP program would be an experimental airplane, designated the X-30, that would demonstrate all of the technologies needed to take us into the era of hypersonic vehicles and aerospace planes.

In the almost 100-year history of airplanes, there has always been a special place for experimental aircraft. Although never designated as such, the first airplane flown by the Wright Brothers was an experimental airplane. The 1903 Wright Flyer was definitely an experiment since the Wrights were not at all sure if it would fly. Since all experimental airplanes are designated by an X, and considering that the Wright Flyer was the original airplane, its designation might logically have been the X-0. Officially, the experimental airplane terminology only began with Chuck Yeager's flight of the Bell X-1. That aircraft, which broke the sound barrier, started the numerical sequencing, and it has continued to this day.

Over the past fifty years, we have seen the rocket-powered X-15, which achieved hypersonic speeds, the X-24 lifting body, and the experimental forward swept wing X-29. It was reasonable, therefore, that the NASP program use the X-30 to demonstrate its technologies.

Besides the focus, the X-30 became the trademark of the NASP program. It provided a vision for the program, a benchmark to measure change, a tool to record progress, and a target to shoot at. If the picture had been a serious engineering drawing, the program would have failed long ago because any changes would have been viewed with alarm. But since it is a concept, and an experimental one at that, it has become the "vehicle" used to focus the efforts of the team while still allowing them great latitude to come up with creative solutions to extremely difficult problems. Two examples might suffice to explain how the open-ended focus of the X-30 has stimulated breakthroughs in technology.

In order to build an airplane capable of flying Mach 25, materials had to be developed that would withstand the tremendous temperatures and huge structural forces of hypersonic flight. In addition, these materials had to be extremely lightweight and capable of being fabricated into almost paper-thin sheets. Finally, they had to be compatible with very hot air (+3000° Fahrenheit), as well as with very cold liquid hydrogen (–450° Fahrenheit). For many years, the NASP program was ridiculed because of its search for "unobtanium," a material that didn't exist.

Five years after the program's initiation, not one, but a number of materials were developed that satisfied the requirements of an aerospace plane. While a tremendous collaborative effort certainly contributed to this breakthrough, it was the X-30 that provided the stimulus for the breakthrough. As various material possibilities were defined, their characteristics were tested against their performance in a potential X-30 vehicle. Since the X-30 vehicle was loosely defined, very different materials and material combinations could be examined. Such broad parametric variations would not have been allowed in a more stringent, prototype aircraft development program. Out of the thousands of different possibilities, three classes of materials emerged as winners. Not surprisingly, none of these had ever been used on airplanes before. The solution was to use a titanium metal-matrix composite structure, thermally reinforced by a carbon refractory composite heat shield, all encompassing a graphite-epoxy fuel tank. In order to accommodate these materials, the shape of the X-30 had to be completely redesigned from a long, thin, cylindrical vehicle to a short, flat, rectangular system. Without that kind of design flexibility, the new materials could never have been used. But without the focus of the X-30, the materials could never have been developed.

Perhaps the most challenging technical aspect of the NASP program has been the development of engines to propel the aircraft from takeoff to orbit insertion. Besides having to span the regime from Mach 0 to Mach 25 and altitudes from sea level to 300,000 feet, the engines must be extremely efficient and lightweight. This necessitated using atmospheric air as the oxidizer for the hydrogen fuel and creating an engine that would be flexible enough to change shape as it traversed the broad Mach number and altitude range. In addition, it had to withstand temperatures of 4,000° Fahrenheit, deal effectively with slush hydrogen fuel, and typically "mix-burn-and-eject" its propellants in less than a few milliseconds. As with the development of the materials, hundreds of engine concepts were designed, and dozens of engines were built and tested.

The criterion used to evaluate an engine concept was always its performance in a potential X-30 experimental aircraft. The team came up with a very simple way to measure the merit of any engine design. After the engine concept was integrated into the design of the X-30, the airplane was "flown" on a computer. If the engine was not efficient or if the engine was very heavy, a large amount of fuel was required to allow the plane to reach orbit. This resulted in a very big takeoff gross weight (the weight of the airplane fully fueled on takeoff). Lightweight, high-performance engines resulted in lighter "paper" airplanes, and they made it to the top of the list in the selection process. After thousands of X-30 designs and computer flight simulations, an engine design was selected that was both feasible and capable of powering a lightweight X-30 into orbit. That engine has now been tested and gave us another breakthrough needed for the NASP program. By using the X-30 to focus the development of the engines, the team was able to come up with a propulsion system that satisfied all of the incredibly challenging criteria of the NASP program and still resulted in a lightweight aircraft. And even though later pictures of the X-30 changed tremendously from the sleek, long, red, white, and blue X-30 of 1986, the plane is still drawn with the engines on the underside. If another engine breakthrough is required, we can still do it without perturbing the concept of the X-30.

Principles

One of my friends is a psychologist who uses hypnosis extensively in his therapy. He is convinced that if a person can be made to concentrate very hard on one single thing, the mind will become very open to external suggestions. He has been able to use this basic principle of hypnosis to help many of his patients do things that they never thought were possible, like quitting smoking, losing weight, and making major changes in their lives. For him, the concept of open focus is a powerful technique to achieve change, sometimes incredible change, in the lives of his patients.

To some extent, leaders must also be psychologists. After all, they are supposed to help, to motivate, to empower, to encourage, and to guide their teams. Good leaders should listen to their followers, they should nurture their teams, and they should try to make them the best that they can be. Sounds like psychology to me! That doesn't mean that leaders need to be certified counselors or hold degrees in psychology (although that might have helped me in a lot of situations). It also doesn't mean that leaders should play mind-games with their people. But it does make sense that leaders use appropriate tools and techniques to achieve high performance in their organizations. If open focus allows individuals to achieve great positive change in their lives, then it should also help teams succeed when change and creativity are required to achieve their goals. Without resorting to hypnotic psychology, leaders can focus their organizations on crystal clear principles, goals, or concepts while encouraging and suggesting the development of creative and innovative approaches.

One of my favorite bosses was occasionally criticized for his seemingly casual, almost loose, management style. Whenever he took over an organization, he would carefully decide the most important goal that he wanted to achieve during his expected tenure. From then on, he would focus most of his, and the organization's, energy on achieving that single goal. Whenever someone suggested an initiative, he would ask them if it made a contribution to the goal. If it did, he would approve it, regardless of how big or little it was or how ordinary or unique it happened to be. After a while, everyone in the organization understood two things. As long as it contributed to the goal, there was a very good chance that the boss would approve the suggestion. And as long as it contributed to the goal, the boss was open to almost any idea. Once everyone realized that this was the modus operandi, unbelievable progress occurred, and remarkable breakthroughs were achieved. General Mike Loh was able to transform the Aeronautical Systems Division into a total quality organization in two years, just by using this principle of open, operation-focused objective. He went on to do the same thing with even larger segments of the United States Air Force. Many other senior leaders are doing the same thing with their organizations: changing the culture to total quality through an unwavering commitment to quality, while empowering their employees to be creative.

Open focus is a powerful tool. It works at the personal level. You probably use it yourself in difficult situations, although you may never have defined it as such. It works at the individual level; ask anyone who has made some significant changes in their lives. It works at the organizational level: examine the operation of some of America's best companies. It even works at the national level; just look at Japan from 1970 to 1990. Doing two opposing things at the same time is not as hard as you think, as long as you're ready for some creativity. My daughters could never walk and chew gum at the same time. But they had no trouble dancing while they were chewing gum.

The greatest thing in this world
is not so much where we are,
but in what direction that we are moving.

—Holmes

CHAPTER 4

Competitive Collaboration
The Vehicle

Every morning in Africa, a gazelle wakes up.
It knows it must run faster than the fastest lion or it will be killed.
Every morning, a lion wakes up.
It knows it must outrun the slowest gazelle or it will starve to death.
It doesn't matter whether you are a lion or a gazelle.
When the sun comes up, you'd better be running.

—Author Unknown

A friend of mine, who is an arbitrator, always reminds me that if everyone agreed, life would be boring. Of course, he would also be penniless. But that old saying suggests that it's the differences that push us into new areas, force us to grow, and broaden our horizons. Fortunately, people don't always agree, so life isn't boring. In fact, everyone is different, and that, as the other saying goes, is what makes the world go round. It also makes for some great breakthroughs.

Harnessing conflicting and competitive energy and turning it into a collaborative force is the dream of every football coach, civil engineer, fifth grade teacher, big city politician, union plant manager, and international statesman, to name just a few. When the competition of ideas and viewpoints yields to collaboration and synergism, breakthroughs do occur. Yet, our inclination is to avoid or sidestep this powerful process. Let's be honest; we usually look for similarities and consensus, and we shape our teams and our lives by surrounding ourselves with people who agree with us. It makes life easier, but it doesn't produce much innovation.

History is full of examples where the melding of different approaches resulted in a breakthrough solution. Perhaps the most famous, near-term example was the 1991 Desert Storm activity that coalesced the forces of such different countries as the United States, Israel, Saudi Arabia, Turkey, Greece, France, and Germany under the team leadership of such different individuals as President Bush, Secretary Baker, Secretary Cheney, General Powell, and General Schwartzkoff. Who would have believed that such a collaboration would have ever been possible, let alone result in a magnificent military and political victory. Competitive collaboration has also been practiced by the Japanese to achieve international economic dominance in markets that used to be totally the domain of other countries. By combining the talents of their highly competitive industrial companies and integrating them through government direction and resourcing, they have achieved breakthroughs with remarkable speed and efficiency.

Competitive collaboration, whether directed or spontaneous, is a major factor in many innovations. While its misuse can lead to chaos and failure, its proper application and management are a powerful vehicle for breakthrough leadership.

Marriage

One of the questions I always ask participants who attend my breakthrough experience workshops is, "How long did the breakthrough experience last?" With thousands of responses in the data base, I've concluded that most of these activities span time periods from several months to several years. Rarely are they shorter than one month or longer than five years. A few years ago, however, I was working with a group of seventy people who had just spent two hours in breakout groups of five sharing a synopsis of their experiences. When the groups returned to the main room, we discussed the key characteristics of their experiences and eventually talked about their time spans. A show of hands revealed that about half the group had experiences that lasted longer than six months. By focusing on an experience span of five years or more, the group reduced to only three people. Ten years narrowed it to one elderly gentleman, who I was sure would lower his hand when I said fifteen years. Not only was his hand still raised at fifteen, it remained up at twenty, twenty-five, even thirty years. Rather than prolong the exercise, I asked him to tell us the length of his experience. "Thirty-seven years," he announced proudly. "And what was the nature of the experience?" I asked. "My marriage," he beamed, "it's been one continuous breakthrough experience all these years." The other participants were a bit stunned; first, they laughed, and then, they became very quiet. After a few seconds, one woman started applauding, and we all ended up cheering and congratulating our dead-serious colleague. After that revelation, I couldn't help probing the other side of the spectrum. Again, we quickly moved to experiences of one month or less, and at one week, two hands remained. One day broke the tie, and once again, I asked for the exact duration. With a bit of a grin, the young man asserted, "Seven minutes, and it was terrific." I never asked the obvious question, but we all wondered if somehow this very short experience might not be intimately related to the thirty-seven-year breakthrough.

Now how could anyone consider marriage, let alone a long, thirty-seven year marriage, a breakthrough experience? Certainly there is challenge, and its very nature implies commitment. At the beginning, many might call it an adventure. As time passes, flexibility and openness are probably necessary if it's to be successful. All of these attributes are certainly present in many happy marriages. But it's a unique combination of competition and collaboration that makes many marriages exciting. In fact, it's these very elements that bring many couples together in the first place. The dichotomy of personalities generates the excitement and the intrigue which sometimes leads to that incredible breakthrough that we call marriage. In spite of all the advice that friends and relatives give us, it's the differences in that significant other that really fascinate us, and it's the challenge of these differences that often leads us to the altar. Competitive collaboration is at work in all marriages. In the most successful ones, its practice is an art form and it often leads to an almost continuous string of breakthroughs. As our thirty-seven-year veteran told the rest of the class, "It's been exciting from the start. She keeps me on my toes."

A second exercise I often use in workshops is a simple creative style inventory labeled IDEA. By selecting self-descriptive words from a series of multiple-choice possibilities, participants classify themselves in one of four categories. The **Interpersonal (I)** types are friendly, empathetic, feeling, supportive, and nurturing. The **Directed (D)** types are visionary, driven, reflective, conceptual, and focused. The **Evaluative (E)** types are analytical, organized, logical, orderly, and structured. The **Assertive (A)** types are confident, forceful, aggressive, impatient, and action-oriented. While this classification can only serve as a very general guide to our creative styles and not as a categorization, it is useful to discuss the forces at work in interactive creativity. In any large class, there are relatively equal numbers of participants in each category, and it is interesting to have them assemble into groups based on their common style. The conversation is usually lively, and they generally reach consensus on those characteristics that differentiate them from the other three groups. There's the predictable competitiveness and good-natured kidding between groups, but most reach the conclusion that you need some of each type to form a creative team. The **I** types provide the "people" emphasis, the **D** types are concerned about the direction, the **E** types insist that it makes sense, and the **A** types stir up the pot. After spending some time in their own groups, four-person **IDEA** teams (one from each type) are formed and given challenging problems to solve.

Invariably, several participants will approach me during the break and ask if they could have an extra copy of the **IDEA** questionnaire to use with their spouses. I always oblige, then I usually challenge them to predict where their spouse will end up among the four categories. Without even reviewing the questionnaire, most of them know exactly which group their spouse is in. Ninety percent of the time, it is not the category that they are in. Often, their spouse's creative style is the very opposite of their own. If the participant is analytical, organized, and logical, the spouse is flexible, artistic, and intuitive. If the participant is reflective, thoughtful, and a planner, the spouse is spontaneous, impulsive, and a doer. Often, one is concerned about feelings, the other about facts. Opposites do seem to attract, and when they make a list of the differences between them and their spouses, they are often amazed. Nevertheless, most agree that these differences make their marriages exciting (and creative) and that they are happy about the situation. While many admit that the differences do lead to some arguments, they have learned to use the differences in positive ways.

While no one ever labels marriage competitive collaboration, that's exactly what it is. Competition of ideas, viewpoints, and perspectives, hopefully within a collaborative, cooperative situation. And it does make for breakthroughs—sometimes six-pound, four-ounce, little blue-eyed ones.

The Artificial Intelligence Applications Center

As any salesman knows, there's a big difference between having a great product and getting someone to buy that product. The same is true for technology. Sometimes the most exciting technologies, the ones that seem to have the most potential, never get incorporated into products or services and, therefore, never get used. In the late 80s, we faced that dilemma in the area of artificial intelligence. Here was a technology, whose very mention inspired creative thinking, ready to be applied but going nowhere fast. Everyone in the advanced systems business was talking about it, but nobody was doing anything to incorporate the technology into their systems. When we analyzed the situation, we discovered the reason for the problem. There was a huge gap between the people who were developing the technology and the people who might use the technology. Unfortunately, there was no one working very hard to close that gap or build a bridge across the chasm. In the sales analogy, there were well-informed suppliers and eagerly anticipating customers, but they weren't talking to each other. And, in the high-tech world of artificial intelligence, salesmen didn't exist. A group of us were challenged by the situation and decided to see if we could solve the problem. We set a target deadline of six months to come up with a feasible solution and spent the first two months trying to understand the technology.

Artificial intelligence is not as mystical as it sounds. It's basically a branch of computer science that incorporates human thinking processes into its operation. There are two main areas of artificial intelligence which have been receiving the most attention: expert systems and pattern recognition. Expert systems are computers and their software systems that incorporate some human experience or knowledge into their processing. Let's say you take your automobile to a service shop because it isn't operating properly. When you get there, the service manager asks you a few questions about the automobile, measures a few things, and listens to the way the engine sounds. He then goes to a computer, inputs all of the data that he collected, and waits for the computer to tell him what's wrong. The computer takes the data and compares it to one million cases of engine malfunction that service managers from all over the country have fed into its data bank. The data from your car matches that of 3,500 cars, 85 percent of which were caused by spark plug misfiring. The computer prints this out and the service manager tells you that you need new plugs. The expertise of all of those service managers was applied to your problem through the computer—hence, the term "expert systems."

The second area of pattern recognition is also straightforward. While most of us think that our brain operates just like a computer, it really doesn't. If it did, we would all be described by words like "slow," "simple-minded," or "dense." If we had to compute all the outcomes every time we had to make a decision, we would be immobilized. We would never be able to drive in traffic or walk down the stairs. Our brains operate by using pattern recognition. If we see a pattern that is familiar to us, we use our accumulated historical knowledge to make some assumptions about the situation. If we see a woman with very long hair, we make the assumption that she has ears under her hair, and we talk to her. A computer might not. Getting computers to use the mechanisms that our brain uses is a very difficult task, but that's what pattern recognition is all about.

After our two-month tutorial in the technology, we started talking to the artificial intelligence hardware and software technologists. We discovered two interesting things. First, most of them loved their work, worked very hard at it, and liked to work independently, and if they did collaborate, they did so with their fellow researchers. Secondly, they were not at all interested in spending their time trying to get people to understand the application of their technology.

We crossed the gap and began interviewing people from a wide variety of industries, businesses, and service organizations who might be able to use artificial intelligence. Actually, almost any area is fertile ground for artificial intelligence, but we focused on companies that dealt with airplanes, automobiles, transportation, education, banking, medicine, energy systems, and engineering support. Occasionally, we would encounter someone that was actually interested in applying the technology to their area. Most of the time, we got blank stares, shrugs, or puzzled looks. In general, people thought that artificial intelligence was one or more of the following: very expensive, too immature, too complicated, scary, or magical. Naturally, there was not much interest in applying the technology to their operations. In the few cases where there was motivation, they had a hard time finding anyone to talk to. And, if they did, they couldn't be understood.

After the interviews, it didn't take a rocket scientist to figure out the problem or the solution: communication. The challenge was how to bring it about. We talked to the government folks; they didn't think that they had a problem. The technologists were a little concerned about the lack of application of their technology, but as long as they were funded, they didn't care. The potential users were occasionally interested in the payoff, but since they had existed until then without it, they were not panicking. After we told them about the Japanese, they looked a little more worried. The college professors thought that bridging the gap was worthy of their attention. Given some curriculum revision, and a few years or decades, they might be able to help. We told them we had three months to go, and they told us to go. Shaken, but not beaten, we returned to our offices and brainstormed for two days. A potential solution began to emerge. We made some calls, set up a few meetings, gave some briefings, and worked out some deals. Two months later, we unveiled the details of the Artificial Intelligence Applications Center to several senior Air Force generals, three

Fortune 100 CEOs, five community leaders, and the presidents of four local universities. Since they had been well-prepared by their staffs, they bought the concept and were all present for the groundbreaking ceremony of the center a month later.

The Artificial Intelligence Applications Center (AIAC) is an organization with the singular purpose of applying artificial intelligence technology. Headed by a retired Air Force general with an extensive technology background, the center is jointly funded by the Air Force and industry through grants that allow specific applications to be explored. The AIAC is under the governance of a board of directors whose membership includes the four college presidents, an Air Force general, and several industrial representatives. Besides studying the applicability of artificial intelligence technology, the center also sponsors courses and workshops, acts as a catalyst between interested parties, and generally serves as the link between the suppliers and the customers. In essence, it fills the gap between those who generate the technology and those who can use it. Since its inception, it has facilitated hundreds of artificial intelligence applications, expanded its operations into other geographical areas, and significantly raised the level of understanding on both sides of the gap. While it is a clear success in its own right, it has also stimulated the use of government, industrial, and academic partnerships as solutions to other technology transfer problems. In a sense, it is also catalyzing the application of some real intelligence, namely competitive collaboration, to the solution of some very difficult problems.

Paper Airplanes

Imagine that you are handed the following package of materials in a 10" × 12" brown shipping envelope:

- six sheets of $8^{1}/_{2}$" × 11" bond paper in assorted colors

- four cheap ballpoint pens

- six paper clips

- four 2" × 4" yellow post-it-notes

- two large rubber bands

- one roll of scotch tape in a plastic disposable dispenser

Your task is to (1) find three other people who are in occupations or professions that are different from each other's and from your own; (2) form a team with these people and give the team a name; and (3) use the materials that you were handed to build an airplane. You will only be allowed twenty minutes to complete the activity, and at the end of that time, you must be prepared to have your airplane compete against several other airplanes created by similar teams with similar materials. The competition will be based on four criteria:

1. the attractiveness of the airplane,

2. the creativity embodied in the airplane,

3. the clever utilization of all the materials you were given, and

4. the distance that the airplane can fly when hand-launched.

Each criterion will be graded on a scale of 1–10, with ten being the best score obtainable. So, your goal should be to achieve a score as close to forty as possible.

Does this sound like fun? Well, it should, because that's how it started out. But, it's turned out to be so much more. And I've got 1,000 paper airplanes in my basement to prove it.

It all began as a cheap way to entertain twenty-four young women from several local high schools who were pretty bored by a long day of technical presentations on aircraft subsystems. I had been asked by a friend to orient and educate these would-be scientists and engineers on the realities of aerospace engineering. Since I have a daughter who became an engineer, I was excited by the possibility of influencing some women to enter a heavily male-dominated field and provide my daughter with some potential soulmates. As technical director of the Air Force Laboratories at

Wright-Patterson Air Force Base, I had access to some of the most advanced facilities and world-class experts in the aerospace field, and I was confident that I could organize a one-day program that would be interesting and educational for the young women.

When they arrived at my office at 8 A.M. on the scheduled day, I told them that we would be visiting over ten different laboratories and that they would receive twelve separate briefings during the course of the day. The briefings would end at 3:30 P.M., and I had left one hour for questions before the bus picked them up to return them to their schools. We moved them out smartly using six second lieutenants as escort officers. They never stopped for the next seven hours, except to take time out to eat lunch. When the students and the lieutenants returned to my office at 3:30, the young ladies looked pretty dazed. I had definitely overdone it. They were totally saturated, and their minds had gone blank. When I asked for questions, no one said a word. The silence was deafening. After several minutes, I let the students relax and met with the lieutenants. If we couldn't get them to talk, what could we do with them for the next hour? One of the officers had just been involved in the annual paper airplane contest at the base, and he suggested that we get the gals to make paper airplanes. I sent the lieutenants scrounging for some materials, and within ten minutes, we had created an exercise that was very similar to the one described at the beginning of this section. Rather than mixing them up by occupation, we forced students from different schools to team up. Otherwise, the same tasking and criteria were used with the students.

The reaction of the students to our off-the-wall improvisation was fantastic. They came alive, and every single one of them threw themselves into the activity with great enthusiasm and sincerity. The six teams, each with a lieutenant as a monitor, congregated in separate parts of our conference room and busily began designing, fabricating, flight testing, and modifying an amazing variety of paper airplanes. Twenty minutes later, they proudly displayed and flew their airplanes for a group of judges that had been quickly commandeered for the occasion. A winner was chosen, and there were continuous celebrations by all of the students until the bus arrived to take them home. As they departed, I breathed a sigh of relief and sincerely thanked the lieutenants for the suggestion and help.

Several days later, I received a thank-you note from my friend, along with the students' evaluation of their day at the base. There was unanimous agreement among the young women; the paper airplane exercise was the most educational and inspiring of all of the activities that day. Even more surprising, three of the students said that this exercise had convinced them to pursue studies in engineering, which they hoped would lead to a profession in the aerospace field. Also attached was a note to me signed by all of the young women. In it they wrote that the exercise really let them see the value of working together in teams and the ability of the teams to come up with some pretty interesting ideas. It was hard to believe; the formal briefings had probably cost a hundred times more than the airplane exercise, but this simple little game was the one thing that they remembered.

Not one to look a gift horse in the mouth, I've now subjected thousands of people to the airplane exercise. Amazingly, almost everyone has the same reaction as the young women. It really teaches them about the power of a team to come up with creative ideas. The more different the people, the more creative the team, and I've seen some of the most amazing aircraft designed and built in less than twenty minutes. Your intuition might lead you to believe that most of the airplanes look like the kind you would make by folding a paper down the center and shaping the front into a point and the back into wings. Well your intuition would be very wrong. Let me tell you about some of these interesting little airborne creations.

First of all, the most creative paper airplanes do not come from teams of aeronautical engineers. Actually, their creations are pretty standard, almost predictable. The most "elegant" solution came from a team composed of a lawyer, a secretary, an accountant, and a production manager. After discussing the situation for eighteen minutes, the secretary picked up the envelope, put all the materials in it, wrote AIRMAIL on the front of the envelope, sealed the envelope, and flung it across the room like a frisbee. It got "10s" in creativity, material utilization, and distance, and won the contest with points to spare.

Most teams create very elaborate airplanes, using some of the materials in very innovative ways. The plastic from the tape is sometimes used to create a cockpit, which is usually suggested by the member of the team with the strongest interpersonal orientation. The artistic members of the team often use the pen and the colors to improve the appearance of the airplane. I've seen some spectacular "nose art" on these airplanes that would rival the World War II bomber variety. The "analytical" members of the team are the ones who usually worry about planning and scheduling, and they keep the team organized to the task. And team members who are in active occupations generally run around making prototypes and flight testing the models. By combining their talents, the teams come up with some fascinating airplanes, and I often bring them back to show to the aeronautical engineers at the base.

The only team that ever scored forty points was probably one of the most diversified teams that I've encountered. The foursome consisted of a fifty-year-old ballet dancer, a forty-year-old psychiatrist, a high school basketball player, and a twenty-seven-year-old electrical engineer. They built the most attractive plane that I had ever seen, with great details and elaborate markings. They used all of the materials, including the envelope and the little piece of metal that is used to sever the scotch tape from the dispenser. The airplane had variable wings and several moving parts, which resulted in a very innovative design. I gave it straight tens in attractiveness, creativity, and material utilization, but it was clear to me that it would never fly more than a couple of feet. The team had sacrificed aerodynamic capability for complexity and beauty. As the "flyers" lined up to compete for distance, this team asked to go last. When their turn finally came, the basketball player crushed the beautiful airplane in his huge hands and flung it clear across the room like a rock—much further than any of their competitors. What else could I do but give them the fourth "10."

A few years ago, a group of Russian aeronautical engineers visited the base, and we became quite friendly. One evening I asked them to take the exercise, and they gladly complied. They took the materials, went into a separate room, and came back twenty minutes later proudly displaying their airplane. It was a miniature replica of a MIG-21, complete with markings and detailed characteristics. They had used only two sheets of paper, and they admitted that it couldn't fly very far. But they were very comfortable with their submission. After all, it was identical to what they were used to seeing in airplanes. Nothing different, just like what they were told an airplane should look like.

The National Team

In the early stages of the NASP program, it was decided that American industry had to assume a leadership role in the development of the aerospace plane. At that time, very few individuals in industry were involved in research and development in hypersonic technologies. Although the United States had a very strong industrial technical base in this area throughout the 50s and early 60s, the cancellation of many advanced-development aerospace vehicle programs in the mid-60s and the emphasis on more mundane technology programs that would assist our efforts in Vietnam significantly eroded our capabilities in hypersonics. In 1985, there were only several hundred scientists and engineers in the United States conducting work in this area, and most of these individuals were scattered among a dozen government centers and several small universities.

In order to develop the technologies and eventually build an aerospace plane, the government program directors estimated that a pool of several thousand experienced engineers, scientists, and program managers would be required. The task was to evolve this manpower base as quickly as possible within the limited government funding that was available to the program. Since funding in 1985 and 1986 was projected to be about $50 million/year, government funds would only have supported a total of 500 people. The solution to the dilemma was obvious: get industry to support the program with their own resources and build up the manpower base in that way. The technique that was used to stimulate this response was the tried and true American approach—competition.

All of the aerospace industry was invited to participate in a four-year competitive program that would lead to the selection of a single contractor to build and fly the experimental X-30 demonstration aircraft. The government would provide some assistance in the form of money, facilities, and technology during the competitive years, but the companies had to fund the bulk of their activity. The carrot was the follow-on X-30 program, which would be fully funded by the government to the tune of several billion dollars.

It was a reasonable approach, and the aerospace industry, still enjoying the profits and expansion of the Reagan military buildup, jumped at the deal. The key aircraft players were Boeing, Lockheed, McDonnell Douglas, General Dynamics, and Rockwell, and the engine competitors were General Electric, Pratt & Whitney, and Rocketdyne. Together, these eight companies represented almost 90 percent of the aerospace industry, so the resulting industrial base would certainly be capable of taking on the X-30 development work.

For the first two years, this strategy served the program very well. Because of the competition and the potential prize, the juices were flowing in each of the companies. Significant money was being allocated, people were volunteering from other sectors of the company for the NASP programs, and top-level corporate management was seriously involved. Whenever I would visit one of the companies, the CEO would take time to chat with me, and enthusiasm was high. Each company had its own NASP logo, hats, T-shirts, banners, anything that made them distinguishable from the competition. All of this was actually very empowering; the competition fed the spirit, and the spirit kept everyone working hard. It was a little hokey, but it was a small price to pay for the resulting output. Meanwhile, the national hypersonic resource base kept growing. By 1987, there were about 2,000 people working on NASP, mostly funded by the companies. At the end of the competition in 1989, the government had spent $600 million while industry had contributed over $800 million. We did a head count in September 1989, and there were 4,800 people involved in the NASP program at that time. If the manpower base was a measure of success, then the competitive strategy of NASP between 1985 and 1989 was a singular success. But there was a price that we paid for this success.

By 1987, each of the competitors had developed integrated teams to work on the NASP program. Using the X-30 as the focus, they had separately evolved their own specific X-30 conceptual design, and they each were attempting to develop the technologies that would be needed for that design. In a sense, there were fifteen distinct NASP programs under way in 1987, since each of the five airframe contractors had cooperative agreements with each of the three engine contractors. Because of the rules agreed to in 1985, these fifteen programs were completely separate from each other; competition-sensitive procedures were followed, and no contractor knew what its competitors were doing. Only the government knew what was going on at all eight companies, but it could do very little to influence the process.

Because of the contracting arrangements (fixed-price contracts were awarded to all eight companies in 1985), the government could watch what was happening, but it could not direct or even suggest any changes to the activity. Even worse, the government found itself almost unable to contribute its own expertise to the contractors. Since a contractor's ideas could not be shared with a competitor, the government usually found itself bound by the information that it had from competing contractors and was unable to even engage with the industry. Unfortunately, most of the real expertise in hypersonics existed in the government from 1985 to 1987, so some of the best ideas never made it to the industrial teams. Only the information that was completely generic could be passed on and that turned out to be a small fraction of what was available from the government. All of the government researchers feared any accusation of contractor "leveling," so their retort was to distance themselves from the contractor teams. In a sense, the government became a sixteenth team, but it never could be a contender to win the competition. The ultimate frustration in the NASP program office was watching one of the contractor teams heading down an erroneous path and not being able to tell it about its dilemma.

While the competition had produced the desired manpower effect, it clearly had shortcomings in terms of information flow and government assistance. If those had been the only drawbacks, then we might have lived with the situation until 1989, declared a winner, and gone on with the X-30 effort. But there was a much more serious issue—it was clear by 1987 that we would never be allowed to initiate the X-30 program in 1989. It was obvious from simple mathematics that we did not have the required critical mass to develop the technology required for the X-30. Even with the significant contractor funding, the NASP program was spending about $200 million/year on technology development. However, the funding had to be divided by sixteen in order to support all the separate efforts. Accounting for overhead, this translated to about $10 million/year/team, enough to do broad-based R&D, but completely insufficient to generate the breakthroughs required for NASP. The result was that everyone was feverishly competing for something that would never come. The win/lose competitive strategy was slowly turning into a lose/lose outcome.

The point was forcefully brought home after the first major review of the program. As is typical with major government programs, an outside team of experts made up of people from government, academia, consultant firms, and think-tanks is asked to review the program to assess its direction, progress, and probability of success. In 1987, the Defense Science Board (DSB) conducted an in-depth review of NASP and concluded that it would never be able to develop the requisite technologies for an aerospace vehicle. In its summary, it particularly focused on the lack of government technical participation and the glaring deficiencies in the materials and engine technology area. Despite loud protestations by many of the government and contractor people involved in the program, they were right. Something had to be done to change the way we were managing the program, or we would never be successful. That led to the concept of national teaming.

At first, it started with the contractors. For a variety of reasons, two of the airframe companies, Boeing and Lockheed, essentially pulled out of the competition. Although they and General Electric were officially downselected by the government in a purposeful attempt to narrow the team to a more manageable size, it was clear from their performance and declining investments that they wanted out. Subsequent conversations with their top management confirmed that they basically agreed with the DSB conclusion and wanted to get out of a program that was not headed for success. With only five companies left, it was somewhat easier to discuss alternate strategies.

The first step was to form a five-way industrial consortium around materials technology. After the DSB report, everyone knew that no one was making the required progress in materials. Since materials technology was fundamental to the program, something had to be done. After several weeks of discussion, they agreed that the materials area was a discipline that might lend itself to a cooperative effort. Since it is such a fundamental technology, sharing the information would not necessarily damage their competitive positions, as long as everything else in the program was maintained as competition-sensitive. Rockwell and McDonnell Douglas began talking to each other about this approach and, with the government's help, drafted a plan to form a materials consortium among the five contractors and the government to work on NASP materials. The first step was to share information with each other, but only in the specific area of materials. While this may sound timid, it actually was a breakthrough in itself. Competing companies rarely share any information that they have paid for using profits. Since most of the NASP materials work had been funded by the companies, this required some risk-taking by the companies. I remember getting a call from one company vice president informing me with alarm that there were people from one of their competitors in an internal materials review meeting, and asking me if this was illegal. I assured him that cooperation might be unusual in our business, but it was not illegal.

The information-sharing exercise revealed what the DSB had clearly stated, that our materials activity was headed towards Unobtanium. After this step, we came together and decided that the only way to really solve this problem was to share not just information but resources. Each of the companies had been spending about $10 million/year in materials spread across their various teams. With additional government funding of $20 million/year, a concentrated allocation of $70 million/year could be applied to materials. This would greatly increase the effort on specific materials development, perhaps achieving the critical mass required for a breakthrough. Once there was commitment to this concept, we had to resolve how the materials consortium would be managed. In an unusual but welcome spirit of cooperation, the five companies set up a unique steering committee structure and resource allocation methodology that satisfied all parties. McDonnell Douglas was chosen as lead for the effort, and we all jumped into the partnership with a great deal of enthusiasm and optimism.

From 1987 to 1989, the NASP materials consortium spent a total of $140 million on key materials development. Each of the five companies took the lead in one of five high-payoff materials technologies. While all five were not successful, several major materials developments occurred in that time period which were breakthroughs for NASP. In the two-year period, the development of metal-matrix and refractory composites was accelerated by a factor of three or four. Generally, materials take twenty years to evolve from concept to production availability. The materials consortium reduced this period to about five years, a breakthrough in itself. The materials that were developed not only satisfied the demanding requirements of the NASP program, but are now spinning off into the energy, automobile, and construction industries. A recent estimate indicates that the national benefits resulting from the NASP materials program could increase the Gross National Product by as much as $4 billion. The second DSB review of the program in 1992 removed materials from the critical path of the NASP program, citing the tremendous progress made by the materials consortium in obtaining the Unobtanium. In addition, the cooperation of the competitors in the materials area has been praised by numerous government and professional agencies and has resulted in several major awards to the NASP team.

As the success of the materials consortium became apparent, the government and the companies began investigating other areas that might benefit from collaboration. By 1988, we had convinced ourselves that a consortium on subsystems and one on diagnostics made sense. We initiated both of these and progress in the two areas immediately surged. By then, it was obvious that this approach might give the program what it needed, and the thought of converting the entire program into a collaborative effort began receiving serious attention. Since the original initiative started with the government, we hosted a meeting to explore forming a single national team in June of 1988. It was a disaster!

While the companies liked the idea of working together in specific areas, they were very opposed to giving up the competition altogether. Each had invested substantial money in the venture, and they didn't want to surrender whatever advantage they might have. Surprisingly, each thought that it was leading in the competition, and they preferred letting the government select a winner rather than yielding to collaboration. Actually, each company possessed some clear attributes, but choosing a winner would not have been easy. More importantly, most of us in the government were convinced that no one company had all the good ideas and that a simple downselect to one organization might jeopardize the success of the program. After serious analysis, the government became convinced that the only way NASP would succeed was to have all of the contractors collaborate as a single team, strengthened by intense support from the government technical centers. Once we reached that conclusion, we were committed to make it happen.

It took two years. We met with the company directors every month for a year before there was a general agreement to collaborate. We hired facilitators and consultants, and the meetings were long and difficult. During these meetings, the government tried to play the role of catalyst, but there were times when some strong positions had to be taken. The decision to form a joint-venture partnership, the first one of its kind in the United States, was reached in January 1989, and it was achieved through consensus. It took another year to iron out the business arrangements between the contractors and to get the Washington bureaucracy to accept this way of doing business. There were at least a dozen occasions where it could have unraveled, but with the help of some visionary leaders in industry and some courageous risk-takers in the government, we succeeded. A $500 million letter contract was awarded to the still-not-legal, joint-venture partnership in June 1990, and the first competitive collaboration in modern aerospace history became official.

While it took many months for all of the contractor personnel to get comfortable with this approach, everyone worked hard to make it a success. And a success it was. Since its inception, the National Team, which includes the government as a partner, has made breakthrough progress. A new, synergistic single concept of the X-30 has emerged, and it incorporates the best ideas of all of the companies and the government. All duplication has been eliminated, and individuals from every organization are working on cross-company teams in very effective ways. Complete openness is the norm, and the distinction between companies has almost disappeared. There is still competition, but it is competition of ideas, not organizations. The diverse backgrounds and philosophies of the different participants have produced a rich storehouse of ideas to use on the program. After the ideas are heard and discussed, the team chooses the best ones and then collaborates on fleshing them out. It is not perfect; there are still areas for improvement, but the collaboration of the competitive philosophies in NASP is succeeding. Like the aerospace plane, the synergism of these powerful forces will hopefully provide the breakthroughs that are needed for the industry of this country to operate in new ways.

Principles

One of the dreams of any leader is to have the perfect team. Whether you're a supervisor or a coach, everyone who has to make something happen through other people fantasizes about having just the right individuals in the organization. If we could just hand pick our people, everything would be great. There would be no conflicts, everything would run smoothly, and we could make tremendous progress towards achieving our objectives. Maybe that would happen, but I doubt it. And even if it did, how long would it last?

After suffering through a long period of instability in my administrative workforce, I was determined to hire someone who would be dependable. I was overjoyed to find that one of the applicants for the secretarial position was a very competent, middle-aged widow who wanted a steady, long-term job. Three months after we hired her, she married one of the engineers, adopted a baby, and handed me her letter of resignation. Back to the drawing board.

Even if we could populate our organizations with exactly who we wanted, chances are we would still not be satisfied. People are so complex that you never know how things will turn out. But it really is just a fantasy, because most of the time we don't get that opportunity. Most of the time, we inherit the team and all the people in it. We can make changes and bring in new individuals that we think would make a positive difference. But unless we are starting from scratch, we get what we get. And that includes the good, the bad, and the ugly. So what's a person to do?

Make the most of it! Unless the team is extremely small, the strengths required to produce creative solutions to our most difficult problems are probably already present in the organization. The challenge is to identify these capabilities and utilize them for the good of the team. The hardest part of the process may very well be in identifying what you have to work with. It may not be obvious that the marketing supervisor really has a tremendous ability to handle tediously complex situations, not until you discover that he repairs antique clocks in his spare time. You also may not be aware that one of your clerical workers is a natural leader and is actively involved in organizing major community service projects. The quiet engineer in the back room probably doesn't look like a risk-taker, until you find out that he is on a competitive skydiving team. Most teams possess all the characteristics that are needed for breakthroughs and high performance. But most of the time, we don't know it. It takes time and effort to determine all of the strengths of all of your people, but it's like mining for gold. The find is worth all of the work.

Once you know the strengths at your disposal, the next step is to integrate them to produce the desired outcome. The scientific analogy is chemistry, making something new out of several reactants. With sports, it's a winning team. With couples, it's making babies. My favorite, and perhaps the most relevant, analogy is from the old "Mission Impossible" television series. Leafing through his files at the beginning of the show, the leader would select the team for the impossible mission from a thick folder of possible candidates. Each of the candidates had several outstanding capabilities, and the mission would determine the final makeup of the team.

If our mission is to achieve breakthroughs, then bringing different people together to focus on that mission is our job. Each of them will have unique capabilities to contribute to the task and our responsibility is to see that they collaborate on the process. Given the right circumstances, and the right chemistry, breakthroughs will occur. It might get a little messy, and some heat and some sparks might be generated, but the products of the reaction may be just what you need to achieve the impossible mission.

Our chief want in life is somebody who will make us do what we can.
—Ralph Waldo Emerson

CHAPTER 5

Structured Flexibility
The Environment

The race is not to the swift,
nor the battle to the strong,
nor riches to men of understanding,
nor favor to men of skill,
but time and chance happen to them all....

For, to everything there is a season,
and a time to every purpose under the heaven....
A time to break down and a time to build up,
a time to get and a time to lose,
a time to keep and a time to cast away,
a time to keep silence and a time to speak.
—Ecclesiastes 9,3

Our intuitive image of the creative person is the individual who is totally spontaneous, generally disorganized, and thrives in a world of chaos and artistic freedom. I guess we get this from caricatures of Einstein and other famous inventors sitting at messy desks, working in crowded laboratories, and creating through flashes of genius and inspiration. In actuality, even the most abstract innovators are pretty organized individuals. Einstein is quoted as saying that creativity is ninety-nine percent perspiration and one percent inspiration. Edison worked on thousands of approaches before the light bulb was invented. The Wright brothers were extremely methodical, carrying out hundreds of tests and analyses in four different laboratories before attempting to fly. And the technical breakthroughs of today generally involve many people working for long periods of time in the well-equipped laboratories of very hierarchical organizations. So how do we reconcile our intuition with reality? The key is in this concept of structured flexibility.

● We all need structure. If we are not provided with structure, we generally create it for ourselves. We discipline ourselves, we develop routines, we get into habits. We do all this because it allows us to get what we want, and it gives us the freedom to do other things. Every morning, I exercise for 30 minutes, then run for 30 minutes, right after getting up. I really would rather do my exercising at some other time of the day, but the morning ritual assures me that I will get it done. As a bonus, I feel good for the rest of the day. It's a constraining discipline that gives me more freedom in the long run.

Structured flexibility delivers the same result. By providing a structure which results in the greatest flexibility for the team, we can create an environment that stimulates breakthroughs. Similarly, a system which carefully removes all of the obstacles that reduce the probability of breakthroughs will deliver the same results. The focus should be on providing the freedom needed for creative activity by using appropriate procedures, processes, structures, and environmental approaches. This is the area where managers can have a tremendous influence, since many of the organizational aspects of management are under their control. Managers can issue policies and implement processes that provide structured flexibility. If it is not within their jurisdiction, they can fight hard at the boundary of their influence to ensure that their team's progress is not unduly hampered by other parts of the organization. And they can behave in a way that fosters the flexibility of their people.

Like competitive collaboration, structured flexibility requires a balance between opposing organizational and environmental forces. If the goal of achieving breakthroughs guides the process of creating the right environment, the balance can be achieved and the results will be spectacular.

The Nine-Dot Greeting Card

My wife is a shopper, a really great one, and she loves to spend hours bouncing from one store to another. I'd swear that we've been to every major mall in the United States. When I say we, it's with a scowling face because I hate to go shopping. As the saying goes, she lives to shop, and I shop to live, and only if my living is threatened. So I've been forced to come up with creative solutions to this "sharing experience." I have three standard procedures: people watching, reading the newspaper, or browsing through a card shop while my wife does her thing. Depending on the city and the climate, people watching can be very fascinating or fantasizing. Reading is acceptable, but I can do that anywhere. Looking at greeting cards and reading the captions and verses are always a treat. My favorites are the humorous cards, but I usually scan all the categories. Since I'm really a romantic, I can even get into the flowery poetic love notes. Over time, my tolerance level for mall ventures has grown from thirty minutes to several hours, almost in direct proportion to the number of cards available for browsing. I am amazed at the diversity and creativity in the greeting card business. For years, I wondered, "Who really came up with these amazingly creative things?" and "How did they go about doing it?" Well, I found out: creative card companies do it creatively.

While there are some pretty standard procedures used by companies such as Hallmark and American Greeting Cards, they are always searching for new ideas that will lead to a new line of cards. Sometimes they get these ideas from their own card line managers, sometimes from unsolicited outside inputs, and sometimes they are stimulated by the success of a competitive approach. All of these techniques may result in a new line of greeting cards, but success in this business cannot be left to chance. In order to be assured of having a continuous supply of ideas for new greeting card lines, they go outside of their own system. As one manager put it, "If they didn't, their house of cards would fall apart in a year."

This guy has so much personal stuff — you become so familiar to him writing that this dinner (his dinner)

One of the most commonly used techniques is to generate a novel solution by forcing a creative interaction in a constrained setting. A hotel room is rented far from the normal office environment so that interruptions are either completely eliminated or significantly minimized. Five or six people are sent to the hotel, and they cannot return until they have developed a new line. The people are carefully chosen to maximize diversity while providing the skills needed for such a task. A typical team might consist of an artist, a business manager, a writer, a production supervisor, a marketing/sales representative, and a graphic arts specialist. Everyone who is needed to develop a new card line is in the room, and they are supplied with whatever they require, including a little food. But they can't break up until they invent a new line.

While this might seem a little bizarre, it's hard to argue with its effectiveness. One of the leading companies told me that their success rate is better than fifty percent. Usually the team spends only a few days in the situation, never more than a week. Some of their more innovative lines have been developed in this fashion and rarely does the experience not produce something of value to the company. If the ideas that are generated cannot be used immediately, they are recorded for future development and are often used as starting points for a new team. Surprisingly, the team members love the experience, even though it does involve some cramped quarters, long nights, and lots of fast food.

Another interesting technique is the outside input. Evidently, there are many people in this world who are very creative in their communications with friends and loved ones. They come up with amazing techniques to share their feelings with the other person. Clipping a note on a cartoon leads to a humorous card. Stapling a business card on a memo generates a different type of greeting. And there are still poets in this land and plenty of verses left to be written. The greeting card companies receive these inputs and produce the finished products that I love to browse through at the mall.

Obviously, companies that do hundreds of millions of dollars of business every year have some structure and procedures that allow them to produce consistent, high-quality products. But to remain competitive, they must be creative. And creativity requires going outside of the normal boundary conditions. So they do that by being as flexible as possible.

Several months ago, one of my friends in the card business sent me a very unusual little greeting card. It had been tailor-made for me in response to a workshop that I had given at his company. In the workshop, I had asked everyone to take the now-famous nine-dot test, where the challenge is to draw four straight lines through a three-by-three matrix of dots without lifting the pen from the paper. It's a very difficult exercise for most people, and the only way to solve the problem is to extend the lines outside of the nine-dot matrix. Many of the participants had done the exercise, so I challenged them to achieve the same result using only one line. After the usual mental struggle, several people came up with a successful solution, and I added to their solutions by showing them several other approaches that I had witnessed over the years. Basically, the nine dots have to be physically rearranged by folding, ripping, cutting, or crumbling the paper so that a single line will intersect all of the dots. Most people are fascinated by the solutions because they never consider modifying the paper; it's too "outside of the nine dots" for most of us. My friend accepted the solutions, but he later confessed that he didn't like the idea of destroying the paper to achieve the solution.

When I saw his card, I chuckled at his resourcefulness. The front of the card read "How do you connect the nine dots using no straight lines?" When I opened the card, I saw that he had inserted a 3" × 5" sheet of rubber upon which was printed the nine-dot matrix, as well as two arrows in opposite corners labelled "pull here." Sure enough, when I pulled and stretched the rubber sheet, all the dots merged, and they truly were connected. When I let it go, the sheet returned to its normal state. And on the inside of the card were just two words—BE FLEXIBLE. I wondered if he had come up with that in a hotel room.

The Mac

When Steve Jobs decided to build a new computer to compete with IBM's entry into the personal computer market, he had to break all the rules of the game. Although his real target was IBM, he also found himself competing with his own company, Apple Computer. It had been Apple that had brought out the first personal computer under Jobs' leadership. IBM quickly responded, and it appeared that the might and muscle of IBM would soon allow them to dominate the personal computer field. A normal response by tiny Apple would never have succeeded. Apple had only 20,000 employees, and IBM had 250,000 people. So Jobs became a pirate in his own company by setting up an entrepreneurial venture within Apple. The "intrapreneuring" paid off. The Macintosh was created, and the little seedling grew up to become the most successful personal computer ever developed. While the Mac itself was a great success, the Macintosh process was just as interesting. It's a wonderful example of structured flexibility and the creativity that is unleashed when this process is employed.

Bringing several of his most trusted employees with him, Jobs started the Macintosh development in a remote part of the Apple complex. In true pirate fashion, a skull and crossbones banner flew over the Mac team's location, letting everyone know that something different was happening inside. The first thing that the team did was to spend a long time developing a vision of the computer that they wanted to create. While computers are very complex systems made up of microprocessor chips and electric circuits, their vision was not a technical one. They decided that their mission was to build a computer that was warm and friendly, something that people would like to use and something that was fun.

Most of the organizational rules were discarded, and people interacted as partners and collaborators rather than superiors and subordinates. Jobs himself operated as a co-equal member of the team, entering into long debates over the computer and offering his ideas as input rather than direction. As new team members were needed, candidates would be asked to spend a day with the team and were "interviewed" by almost everyone on the project. The key criterion used to determine whether they were hired was not their expertise but their reaction to the vision of the project. If their eyes lit up and they got excited, they became part of the team. If they were only interested in developing a computer, they were not hired. The Mac team was more concerned about the passion rather than the credentials of its members.

As the team began to make progress and the Mac began to take shape, there was great pressure from the rest of Apple to bring the small team into the company mainstream. Since many of the functional skills required to fully develop and shake-out a computer existed in the main company, it made good business sense to integrate the Mac team with the rest of Apple. Jobs, wearing his Macintosh hat, resisted his own company and kept the Mac team as a separate entity. Even after the prototype of the Macintosh was complete, he restricted its exposure and only allowed members of the Mac team to see it.

Production of the Mac caused even greater conflicts. Since the main company was very experienced at producing personal computers, it would have been logical to turn the prototype over to the existing manufacturing capability in Apple. Again, Steve Jobs broke the rules and set up a separate production facility for the Macintosh. Nor would he use experienced computer production managers to run the Macintosh manufacturing facility. Instead, he hired a liberal arts major with organizational development skills to run the Mac production complex. He wanted every aspect of the new Mac computer to be as fresh and as innovative as possible. And he hit the jackpot. While Jobs had set an objective to sell 50,000 Macs in the first three months of production, 130,000 Macintosh computers were sold. Because of its great market success, the Macintosh became the basis for an entire line of Apple computers (generally acknowledged to be the most innovative in the personal computer field). By going around and outside of the mainstream structure and operating with extreme "adhocracy" and flexibility, Steve Jobs was able to deliver a major new product in record time. Enhanced with extraordinary empowerment and visionary leadership, the structured flexibility of the Apple Mac team yielded one of the biggest breakthroughs of the decade.

When I finally decided to write this book, one of my friends suggested that I buy a portable computer. Since I spend so much time on airplanes, the idea made sense. So my wife and I went to one of the giant computer outlets near our home to buy a portable. I came away pretty confused! All of the portable computers, and there were fifteen different makes, looked pretty good, and their prices were very competitive. After attempting to logically analyze the situation for several days, I gave up. I decided to go with my gut. I figured that if I was going to write about breakthrough leadership, I should do it on a machine that itself was a break-through. So I bought a Mac, not the one that Steve Jobs created, but one of its own little descendants. It's a great machine, delivers all that I want, and I bought it for a good price. But it does something else—it inspires me. Every time I get blocked trying to write, I recall the Mac story. Then I put on a paper pirate hat that a waiter at a Long John Silver's seafood restaurant gave me. After a few min-utes, I usually can break through the problem and start writing again. But I'm not as flexible as Steve Jobs; I do take off the hat when I see the stewardess approaching.

Bridging the Gap

By now, I hope that you buy into the idea that, given the right conditions, a team of individuals can come together in a synergis-tic way and generate ideas that are quite creative. The results are very dependent on the individuals involved and their ability to communicate effectively while exploring and utilizing their differ-ent contributions and characteristics. But what about a really big group of people, say, 50 or 100 people. In groups that large, communication at the personal level is quite difficult and the organizational structure needed by such a group may get in the way of innovation. In order to see if big groups can be creative, several large teams of multidisciplined individuals were asked to do something that really stretched their capabilities.

The task was to move a six-pack of pop from one side of the room to the other using only straws, string, paper, and pens. The six-pack was placed on a table whose height was two feet, and it had to end up on another table which was three feet tall. The gap between the tables was about ten feet, and everyone had to stay behind the tables during the transfer of the six-pack. The group was supplied with 100 plastic straws, 20 sheets of large paper, 2 magic markers, and a roll of string. They were given two hours to complete the task, and they were allowed to organize themselves in any way that they wanted. The only other condition was that everyone be involved throughout the exercise.

Watching the various teams operate was as interesting as observing them bridge the gap. Most of the teams started off in the same way. Natural leaders would emerge, subgroups would be organized and tasked with specific functions, and a communication mechanism was established. The team then spent a long time selecting and planning the approach. Once some general consensus was reached, they would start constructing their systems.

Since the six-pack could not touch the floor between the two tables, every team decided to construct some type of bridge and a vehicle in which to carry the cans. Surprisingly, there were as many different bridges and vehicles as there were teams. The key decision was whether the vehicles would ride on top of a span bridge or hang from a flexible suspension bridge. While the teams automatically assumed that the bridge was the more difficult task, the vehicles always turned out to be the critical element.

About halfway through the exercise, every team usually encountered its first crisis. It became apparent that the vehicle would not be able to support the entire six-pack, and every team decided to break it up and reassemble it at the destination. Buoyed by this little breakthrough, they resumed their work of building bridges and vehicles. As the bridge took shape, there was great pressure on the vehicle sub-team to deliver its product on time. At this point, individuals from the bridge team wanted to help the vehicle team, but they really didn't want any help. In the meantime, it was obvious that the specifications for the bridge and the vehicle were not necessarily compatible. That's when the organization generally started to break down.

As tensions grew and adjustments had to be made, the groups underwent various levels of stress and anxiety. They all successfully dealt with this and restructured the sub-teams in very appropriate ways. As the deadline approached, extraordinary efforts were delivered, sometimes in most unexpected ways, by people who came out of nowhere. From afar, the final phases of construction seemed almost chaotic, but not to those involved in the process.

Every team managed to successfully complete the exercise, although with varying degrees of style. One team transferred the last can with twenty seconds to go, while another team eventually moved the entire six-pack across at one time. One team built a span bridge that was so strong that one of the smaller team members was actually able to creep across the bridge and carry the six-pack across. Another team built a tram system that collapsed just after the last can was delivered. Because of their success, every team staged rowdy celebrations with group pictures, bridge dedications, and all kinds of symbolism and loudness. While I'm not sure that any of the approaches would qualify as a breakthrough, all of the teams exhibited genuine creativity despite their large size.

After each team completed the exercise, we always spent about thirty minutes discussing the activity. Most people wanted to talk about content, but it was clear that the process used by the team ultimately determined the level of creativity exhibited by the team. The teams that tried to rigidly stick to their original plans generally had the most problems. They were followed closely by those teams that completely abandoned their organizational structure as soon as they encountered some difficulties. The most successful teams, as measured by their self-appraisal on collaboration and innovation, were the ones that maintained both structure and flexibility. Those teams that felt the best about their performance were able to shift priorities and modify their direction without abandoning the overall vision or their rules of engagement. In those teams, people would move from one subgroup to the other, but only to help and not to direct. Those same teams exhibited a rhythm, almost an ebb and flow, that allowed the team's total energy to be applied to the right thing at the right time. It was this give and take around a singular purpose that was the mark of the more successful and innovative teams.

Upon examination, the bridges and the vehicles of the most successful teams exhibited the same characteristics as the team—structured flexibility. But that shouldn't be a surprise. Good bridges have both structure and flexibility. If they didn't, they would collapse. Good vehicles exhibit the same characteristics. If they didn't, they would break. Without both structure and flexibility, it's hard to bridge the gap, build airplanes, or break limits.

Managing NASP

The concept of a technology development program being sponsored by several government agencies is not new. There have been a number of joint programs over the past fifty years, and some of them have been very successful. Unfortunately, most of them have not. The basic premise underlying all joint programs is very sound. Government organizations with similar needs can share in the support, as well as in the benefits of a joint program. At first glance, they make a lot of sense, and, at least in the beginning, there is usually a strong commitment by all parties to make them work. As time goes on, difficulties arise, and the test of a joint program is how well these difficulties are handled by the partners. The analogy to marriage is hard to resist. The honeymoon is always great, but many marriages end up in divorce. To make matters worse, joint programs can't even count on love to pull them through.

The concept of a technology development program being managed like a major systems program is also not new. The most famous examples in recent times have been the Apollo program, the Space Shuttle development, and the Strategic Defense Initiative (Star Wars) program. Apollo was a great success, the Shuttle had mixed reviews, and the jury is still out on the SDI effort. Generally, technology has to be well-developed before a major systems program is initiated. With a sound technology base, system programs can be managed against cost, performance, and schedule baselines to maximize productivity and minimize cost and schedule overruns. If the technology is not sufficiently mature, program planning is very difficult, and baselines are difficult to establish and maintain. The higher the technology risks and uncertainty, the more difficult the program management challenge. In the extreme case where breakthroughs are required in the technology, breakthroughs may also be required in the management approach.

NASP is a joint program as well as a high-technology, systems-oriented effort. To make things even sportier, there are five government organizations involved in the effort and over 300 separate companies, universities, and government centers developing the technology. Usually, programs of this nature have strong presidential support to carry them through. Apollo and the moon landing were initiated by President Kennedy and fully supported by all of the presidents who served in the 60s. The Star Wars program was initiated by President Reagan and required his, as well as President Bush's, strong support to sustain funding for the program. NASP has received some support from the administration, but it is certainly not a presidential commitment. Over the years, most of the support has come from a loosely aligned coalition of congressmen, staffers, and administration leaders who felt that the eventual promise of NASP was worth its cost. Throughout its history, NASA, the Air Force, the White House science advisor, the vice president, Congress, and the industry have all taken the lead in supporting the NASP program. Because each supporter emphasized a different program approach, the program management needed to be extremely flexible in executing the effort. Simultaneously, a fundamental direction and structure had to be maintained in order to keep the program reasonably stable and financially sound. This necessarily dictated the form and functioning of the NASP Joint Program Office, which was basically one of structured flexibility. Fortunately, this approach has allowed the program to survive at least a dozen major changes in emphasis and direction while maintaining the fundamental vision of the effort and generating the many technical advances that have been required by the program.

From the beginning of the program, the management approach has been responsive to the need for creativity and innovation. This led to the adoption of a very shallow organizational structure, with only one layer of management, horizontal integration, and plenty of opportunity for initiative and creativity from the program personnel. While there are over 700 government people on the program, less than 100 are in the program office. The remainder are scattered throughout the country and have the advantage of utilizing the various government facilities, systems, and support organizations in their locale. After forming the joint-venture partnership, the national contractor team adopted a similar approach, moving less than 100 people to its headquarters in Palmdale, California, while supporting several thousand people in many field locations. This small central core approach, coupled with the loosely integrated structure, allowed great flexibility in the conduct of the program and facilitated rapid response to the numerous financial, organizational, and technical changes in the program.

The foundation for managing the program is a simple roadmap describing the activities that are needed to develop the technology required for the X-30. The plan is reviewed periodically and modified according to the technology progress that has been achieved. How the work gets accomplished is left up to implementing organizations. Over 50 government projects and 100 contractor projects are executed in this fashion, with reviews occurring biannually. While specific "exit criteria" were established to evaluate when and if the program accomplished its objectives, management of the individual efforts is left flexible to encourage creativity. Expertise from every technical center involved in the program is available through quarterly reviews and technical committee meetings. Because so many different disciplines and organizations are involved, the interaction is very synergistic, and great advances have been made in many of the key areas.

Perhaps the loose/tight approach used in the NASP program is best illustrated in the design activity. For the past two years, a basic design for the X-30 has guided all technical activities in the program. Conversely, as technical results are obtained from the technology development programs, they are quickly integrated into the design and generally produce either a positive or negative impact on the eventual X-30 performance. Since early in the program, the key X-30 performance parameter tracked by the program management was the predicted takeoff weight of the X-30 required to achieve orbit (to go from earth to space and return). About every six months, the latest innovations in design and the results of recent technical developments were incorporated into the process, and a new X-30 design was generated. With it came a predicted X-30 takeoff weight that was closely tracked to determine the progress of the contractor and government teams. This resulted in enormous expenditures of manpower, significant perturbations to almost every element of the program, major changes in the X-30 concept, and wild swings in the perception of the program by our supporters and detractors. While no one wanted to give up the design of the X-30 as the fundamental baselining structure of the program, we all began searching for a method which would maintain the flexibility but provide a bit more stability.

In 1991, we modified our design tracking approach by stabilizing the X-30 design at a takeoff weight of 350,000 pounds. At this weight, the X-30 would truly represent a quantum leap in our ability to go into space, considering the Space Shuttle has a takeoff weight of over four-and-a-half million pounds. By declaring that the design was stable around the parameter, we eliminated all the effort required to redesign every six months, and we were able to look at any positive or negative input to the design as a unique change. The tracking criteria became the speed that a 350,000-pound X-30 could achieve, and the resulting speed was tracked relative to the goal value of Mach 25, that speed required to go into space. For example, if a technical result came in less than expected and it resulted in a negative impact on the airplane, its effect would be translated into a velocity deficit (say, 0.6 Mach). Since the goal was still to achieve an overall velocity delta of zero, a search would begin for a design innovation or technical breakthrough that would result in a 0.6 Mach credit. If several credits accrued such that a positive delta existed, we would still not change the design since the next design review would likely require those credits to balance the inevitable deficits of a challenging technical program. By so doing, we were able to track our progress yet provide very specific and focused stimulation for the creative process.

In the early part of 1992, a number of disappointing results in the engine and structures technology efforts resulted in the velocity deficit growing to four Mach numbers; that is, the 350,000-pound X-30 would only be able to achieve Mach 21, way short of space. While many argued that our now standardized approach to solving the program by stimulating some positive velocity inputs would work, we temporarily abandoned this approach in favor of a potentially more innovative solution. A significant number of government and contractor personnel from all over the country were asked to form two teams that would be located in Palmdale, California, for four months to work on this problem. One team, called the Blue Team, was asked to come up with as many solutions as possible to our velocity problem, and they were constrained in only two ways. The Blue Team was to use only the individuals who were originally assigned to their team, and their solution(s) had to be generally accepted by the NASP technical team as feasible approaches. Although constrained, the people on the Blue Team were highly diverse and proven innovators. The Red Team, while smaller, was allowed to supplement their membership with anyone in the world, and their suggestions were only constrained by the laws of physics.

After the allotted time, both teams came up with suggestions that were greater than four Mach numbers. While the Blue Team's solutions were more conservative, there were more of them, and the cumulative result met the goal. The Red Team came up with a mixed bag, a few big inputs that required much more analysis and a number of smaller ones, a few of which were identical to some from the Blue Team. The teams were then combined, and the resulting Purple Team came up with several additional innovations and an overall velocity delta that greatly exceeded the original goal. After an appropriate reward ceremony, the teams were dismissed, and the members were allowed to reintegrate into their respective teams. While it has not been necessary to reinvigorate the design process in such an unusual manner since that time, I am sure that we would not hesitate to reshuffle the system on a moment's notice if it were necessary.

While the conceptual design of the X-30 aircraft uniquely demonstrates what can occur using a flexible approach to a highly structured process, this philosophy has prevailed throughout the program. Conducting research and development is necessarily a highly creative and unconstrained activity. Building an aircraft, even an experimental one, requires a good deal of regiment and discipline. Doing both at the same time has forced a blend of structure and flexibility. The result has provided NASP with the setting needed to meet the challenges of this effort.

Principles

Some time back, I attended a two-day workshop that examined individual creativity from a historical and a developmental viewpoint. There were two interesting conclusions that came out of that study. After discussing over 100 cases where a single contributor

was responsible for one or more major scientific, medical, philo-
sophical, or social breakthroughs, we found that most of the breakthroughs occurred before the contributor was thirty years old.
Secondly, the investigation revealed that the individuals who were
older than thirty when they made their breakthrough were relatively new in the field of the discovery. For example, a scientist
might make a contribution in chemistry before turning thirty and
then come up with a breakthrough in the social sciences later in
life. What the data implied was that the "window" for an individual to make a major creative contribution in his field was
limited. In other words, creative people make their mark early in
their careers. It may very well take several years or more to understand the fundamentals of a discipline, but spending a very long
time in a profession seems to decrease the probability of making a
breakthrough.

Common sense also tells us that there is an optimum time span
for meaningful individual creativity. Little children are extremely
creative since they are not aware of the rules and laws governing
many situations. They will venture into behaviors and circumstances that most adults would avoid, mainly because the children
don't know any better. While this fits the strict definition of creativity, their parents label it somewhere between cute and embarrassing. At the other extreme, senior citizens are usually not the
vanguard of innovation. Their ways have been set by years of
experience and trial and error, and most are interested in stability
and predictability. Somewhere between two and eighty-two lies our
window of creative opportunity. Extrapolating from both ends
suggests that there is a time period in each of our lives when we
know enough to be smart but we don't know enough to be scared.
As the saying goes, that's when we know just enough to be dangerous. When that happens is very dependent on the individual, the
situation, and the circumstances surrounding the situation. If the
situation is new or the circumstances are very challenging, it could
happen at any time. Overall, however, it seems to occur when we
are in transition periods or, rather, just before we make the transition. At these points in our lives, we are uncomfortable with the
way things are, and we want to move on to something else.
Sometimes these transitions are extremely chaotic and abrupt, and
then a major change in our life and lifestyle results. More often, we

make a series of small changes from a present to a future way of living. During these transitions, we modify the structure of our lives. If we are flexible, the transitions can be smooth. If not, they may be traumatic. The difference sometimes is between breakdown and breakthrough.

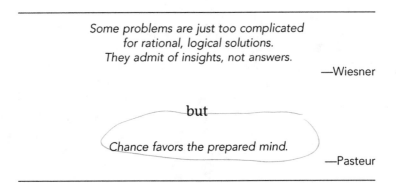

Some problems are just too complicated
for rational, logical solutions.
They admit of insights, not answers.

—Wiesner

but

Chance favors the prepared mind.

—Pasteur

CHAPTER 6

Personal Commitment
The Force

It is not the critic who counts,
not the man who points out how the strong man stumbled,
or where the doer of deed could have done better.
The credit belongs to the man who is actually in the arena;
whose face is marred by dust and sweat and blood;
who strives valiantly;
who errs and comes short again and again;
who knows the great enthusiasms, the great devotions,
and spends himself in a worthy cause;
who, at best, knows in the end the triumph of high achievement;
and who, at the worst, if he fails, at least fails while daring greatly.
—NASP Credo borrowed from Teddy Roosevelt

Breakthroughs are not easy to achieve; if they were, they wouldn't be breakthroughs. The barrier or problem that must be overcome is a very real challenge. The excitement and energy that are stimulated by the challenge will be tempered by failure and disappointment. The shiny vision will be clouded by the atmosphere of reality and human frailty. Collaboration may degrade into conflict and the "system" may not be a friend; it may even be the enemy. It takes great persistence and determination to suffer through

97

these dilemmas, just as it does to achieve anything that is difficult to obtain. In the end, it will come down to commitment. There will be many opportunities to abandon the project, and there will be plenty of people to blame for it not succeeding. There will always be a good excuse to explain away the problem and, as a last resort, you can always claim that there is no solution. But if there is a solution, and if it takes a breakthrough to achieve it, you have to go on. And going on will take commitment.

In the beginning of an exciting activity, there is generally enough spirit to overcome the usual obstacles. As the project stretches and the road gets rougher, the bonding of the team may begin to crack. Individuals may abandon the project or give up the vision. This can shatter a team that has been operating in a highly integrated fashion. Even the leader may opt out of the venture and the team may have to seriously evaluate its future. Any of this will certainly cause a setback, but it doesn't have to end the quest for a breakthrough. If the individual members of the team have personally committed to the goal, then the project will go on. It's at the personal level that commitment is the most powerful because it involves our reputation or our honor. If there is solid personal commitment to the endeavor, only a catastrophe can stop the progress. Personal commitment and faith in the outcome are two of the strongest forces in the world. Breakthroughs need that kind of force; in fact, breakthroughs cannot occur without it.

The Gandhi Button

Almost everyone is familiar with the story of Gandhi. Movies, books, speeches, and anecdotes about Gandhi have immortalized his impact on history. Despite this familiarity, most are still amazed by how one man, one relatively ordinary man, brought an empire to its knees. Perhaps the change that occurred in India was inevitable. Maybe Gandhi was merely the facilitator, the catalyst for this social breakthrough. But the fact is that one person decided that the world had to change and, in the end, the world changed. Gandhi was educated, and he had skills, but he also had faults and limitations like all of us. Retrospective analysis would suggest that he took a stand at the right time, and during his fight, some things went his way. But it wasn't luck, brilliance, power, or even a miracle that made the difference; it was commitment. One ordinary person, armed with commitment, changed a country and then the world. One ordinary person, through persistence and determination, altered the course of history, principally because he decided that it had to be done and he was the guy to do it.

Several years ago, 300 technical managers and senior researchers from the Air Force's Wright Laboratory were coerced into attending an intense two-day workshop on breakthrough thinking. I was the bad guy who did the coercing because I was hoping that this workshop might help shake things up for the better. Most of the attendees were very reluctant to spend two days doing strange, touchy-feely, psychological exercises. After all, these guys and gals were engineers, and this kind of stuff doesn't sit well with engineers. But the commander yielded to my lobbying, and the workshop was approved. The participants, essentially the top four management layers in the laboratory, were directed to attend. In a military organization, people obey direction, and almost everyone showed up. It was clear by then that I was the one behind this crazy idea, and my judgment, if not my reputation, was on the line.

The workshop was very intense, almost theoretical, and challenged many of the premises that most managers and engineers hold dear. By the morning of the second day, I was the butt of many jokes, and it looked like it was going to be a giant fiasco. I must admit that I was very anxious, and if it had been possible, I might have ended the workshop at that point. Charlie Smith, the instructor, convinced me to hang in, and we did complete the entire second day. The focus of that day was on the power of commitment and its relationship to change. Sometime during that day, Charlie talked about Gandhi and his commitment. The story did strike a chord in me, but as I looked around the room, it seemed that most of the folks were bored, eager to leave, or still mad at being forced to attend. The workshop finally ended, and a few of my friends came up to me and said that they thought it was worthwhile. Most said nothing, and about a dozen guys told me that I had wasted their time. But Dr. Joe Shang, a senior scientist who specializes in very sophisticated computational software development, handed me a note as he ran out of the room that

Friday. Joe is a good guy and a brilliant scientist, but he has a thick Chinese accent, and it's sometimes difficult to follow Joe in a conversation. The note said "Going to get Cray, call you Monday." I knew what the note meant, but I couldn't connect it with the workshop or Joe's haste to leave the building.

Joe had been attempting to get the laboratory management to buy a multimillion-dollar Cray super computer for five years. He wanted one to do his work, and the Cray would also be useful to several other researchers in other parts of the laboratory. But politics always got in the way, and the high cost of the computer was used as the excuse to disapprove Joe's request. Over the past year, Joe had solicited my help in his quest. I agreed with his rationale, and I tried to help, but I couldn't get the leadership to put politics aside. There didn't seem to be any hope. The note indicated that Joe saw some hope, but I would have to wait the weekend before Joe got back to me.

Three weeks after the workshop, the Wright Laboratory ordered a six-million-dollar Cray computer for Joe and his colleagues. They did so because Joe had influenced another organization to share the cost of the Cray. That organization was headed by a very influential general who had been convinced that the Cray purchase was critical to the future of his project. The convincing took place from 4:00 P.M. to 8:00 P.M. on a Friday, three weeks earlier. Joe had rushed from the workshop and gone directly to the general's office. The secretary wouldn't let Joe in without an appointment, but he pushed his way through. He jumped in front of the general and declared that he wasn't leaving until his mission had been accomplished. Well, it took four hours, a lot of explaining, and some fancy footwork to keep the general inside his office, but Joe did get the general to buy in. And that got him the Cray computer.

When Joe called me on Monday after the workshop, he was talking so fast that I didn't understand him at all. Every once in a while I could make out a few words, like Cray, Gandhi, and workshop. Joe was still excited by what had happened that Friday night, and I finally decided that the only way that we could communicate was in person. I went to his office, and the story unfolded.

Evidently, Joe was really turned on by the story of Gandhi at the workshop. He kept saying that after he heard the story, it was like someone had pushed a button in his mind. He suddenly realized that he could do things that he once thought were impossible. If he really wanted the Cray computer, it was up to him to get it. And that's exactly what he did.

I asked about his conversation with the general, and he said he didn't remember much of it except for the end, when the general committed to help buy the computer. I had to grin as I conjured up the vision of Joe, attacking with scientific arguments conveyed in broken English, and the general finally surrendering when Joe wouldn't let him go home—almost like Gandhi and the British soldiers. Somewhere in Joe, there's a button that activated intense commitment, and the story of Gandhi pushed that button. Somewhere in all of us, there's a Gandhi button. Push that button, and there's no telling what might result—maybe a breakthrough.

Voyagers and Gossamers

One of the claims that those of us in the NASP program often make is that our airplane will be the first to orbit the earth. While that is true if the orbiting is done in space, it is not really an accurate statement. That was forcefully brought to my attention several years ago by Dick Rutan and Jeanna Yeager. At the time, I had the pleasant task of introducing Dick and Jeanna to a crowd of several hundred people who had come to hear their account of the Voyager program. Right after I handed Dick the microphone, he turned to me and said that I now could retire. Since the Voyager aircraft had just flown all the way around the world without landing or refueling, my mission had been accomplished and there was no longer any need for NASP. He was literally correct, but we both agreed that it would be nice to orbit the earth without worrying about crashing into tall buildings.

Voyager started off as the dream of Dick and Burt Rutan of Mojave, California. Dick was the pilot, and Burt was the engineer. Together, they decided to build an airplane like no other ever built. The goal was to create the first (and still the only) aircraft to make a nonstop flight around the world without refueling. After many years of development and testing, the Voyager was finally completed.

Voyager looked more like a catamaran than an airplane. Two long booms intersected the wings, and between the booms was the canoe-shaped fuselage where a small cockpit/cabin area was located. The engines were mounted in the front and back of the fuselage. Because of Burt's expertise in advanced lightweight materials, the basic structure of the Voyager was a honeycomb of resin-treated paper, surrounded by two layers of carbon fiber cloth that was coated with a hard, strong epoxy covering.

Voyager was designed as one large fuel tank, since it had to carry enough fuel on takeoff to make it all around the world. Sixteen tanks were placed in the very long wingspan, and these tanks fed into the main fuselage tank. The fuselage tank then fed directly to the two main engines through the use of mechanical pumps. During the flight of the Voyager, Dick and his crewmate, Jeanna, had to be very careful when drawing fuel in order to keep the weight in the wings evenly distributed. This was because the wings, made out of the fiber/paper material, were very flexible and susceptible to breaking under uneven loads. Even in normal flight, the wings would bend up and down fifteen feet or more.

The length of the cockpit/cabin area was seven-and-a-half feet long, and it was only two feet wide. Since Dick and Jeanna had to live in this nonpressurized space for more than a week, special measures had to be taken. Jeanna admitted that she cut off most of her hair just before the flight in order to simplify her situation as well as to save weight and volume in the cabin. They both went on stringent diets prior to the trip in order to minimize their body weight as well as the amount of food and water that they had to carry during the voyage.

The flight began early on the morning of December 14, 1986, after almost seven years of preparation. Voyager took off from Edwards Air Force Base in California and headed west. On board was a navigation computer, an autopilot, weather radar, a long-range radio for communications, a small amount of food for the pilots, and as much fuel as they could carry. As the Voyager attempted to lift off, it wavered, and one of the wingtips hit the runway at Edwards, shearing off part of the wingtip. Ordinarily, that would have forced an abort situation, but Dick and Jeanna elected to go on and attempt the flight even with that auspicious start.

Voyager climbed slowly over the Pacific Ocean and headed towards Hawaii. Everything went reasonably well for two days, and the pilots worked very hard to conserve and distribute the fuel while minimizing their intake of the precious food. On the third day, the autopilot suddenly failed. The trip might have ended right then had it not been for a backup unit that Jeanna had carried on board. She quickly installed the unit, averting a potential disaster, and the voyage continued.

As Voyager headed over Africa on the fourth and fifth days, it got caught in some violent thunderstorms and almost came apart. With some terrific flying and a little bit of luck, the plane and crew survived the encounter only to find themselves staring at a towering mountain. Even though it consumed a lot of fuel, Voyager climbed to 20,000 feet to get past the barrier. On the eighth day, they crossed over Costa Rica and then flew again over the Pacific Ocean. On the ninth day, they experienced engine trouble and spent most of the day repairing one engine while the other kept them going. With all of their difficulties, they ended the day wondering if there was enough fuel left in the plane to make it safely back to land.

Finally, with the morning sunrise at their backs, they saw the coast of California. At 8:05 A.M. on December 23, 1986, Voyager landed at Edwards Air Force Base. The nearly 27,000-mile trip had taken 9 days, 3 minutes, and 44 seconds. When Voyager landed, there were 18.3 gallons of fuel left in the tanks, only enough for a few more miles!

When the speech was over and Dick and Jeanna had answered over one hour of questions, I suggested that we head back to the hotel where they were staying. During the drive, I asked them if they could identify a single event or circumstance during the flight that was the critical turning point in the success of Voyager. Dick didn't hesitate.

Special guy that has been in cool too many important places.

- World travel
- Girl
- Crazy Scientist
- Little boys asking questions

Sure, but it wasn't during the flight. It was at the press conference that we called before we finished the airplane. That was really our darkest hour, even with all the problems that we would encounter on the flight. We had run out of money to build the airplane. The technical problems seemed overwhelming, and none of us were sure that we could successfully build and fly the airplane, let alone around the world. So I called a bunch of reporters and told them we had some exciting news to report. They all showed up at Mojave, and I told them that everything was going well and we would be ready to fly on schedule. I added that I was very confident that everything would go fine with the airplane and that we would be able to make it around the world in one shot. It wasn't exactly the truth, but it sure did the trick. After that, none of us would have ever backed out of the project. I would have rather crashed than to explain in public why we didn't make it!

I have often thought about Dick's press conference promise and the power of commitment in driving us to do extraordinary things. From time to time, I've also make some pretty ridiculous commitments, and I've usually felt compelled to see them through, mainly because my reputation was on the line. Occasionally, however, I get carried away and promise something that's so outrageous that I can't deliver. On one such occasion, I decided to call Dick Rutan and ask him for some additional advice on commitments and promises. Since the issue was around the aerospace plane, he suggested that I fly out to Mojave and meet with him and his brother Burt.

As we sat around the modest conference table in Burt's Scaled Composites company office area, I lamented on how tough it was to maintain the government support for the NASP program. They both listened intently and only responded when I told them that the aerospace plane project cost might exceed $10 billion. "Nonsense," said Burt, "you should be able to do it for one or two billion. And you might get most of what you want for free." I couldn't figure out where he was going with this, since we all were aware of the many independent cost estimates that had pegged the cost of NASP at around $10 billion. "Why don't you make it a contest," he said. "Offer a prize of a billion dollars to the first team that successfully builds and flies an aerospace plane. If some group succeeds, you just got yourself a terrific bargain. If no one actually achieves the goal, some tremendous airplanes will be built during the contest, and they won't cost the government a cent."

It was an amazing suggestion, typical of the Rutans, and I knew where it came from. Burt and Dick were good friends with Paul MacCready, who had built the Gossamer Albatross. The MacCready Gossamer Albatross was the first human-powered aircraft to cross the English Channel. MacCready and his team had built the aircraft in response to a prize of 100,000 pounds offered by Sir Henry Kremer for the first human-powered flight across the English Channel from England to France.

The Gossamer Albatross looked like a giant dragonfly with a 93-foot-wide wing span. It was made almost entirely of plastic and supported by styrofoam ribs and steel wire bracing. The pilot sat in a mylar enclosed cockpit, ten feet high and eight feet long. Power for flight was created when the pilot pedaled a bicycle without wheels that was connected to a drive shaft and a propeller. The wing gave the aircraft lift, and the propeller gave it forward motion.

Twenty-six-year-old Bryan Allen, a champion bicyclist, was the pilot of the Gossamer Albatross when it made its historic flight on June 12, 1979. At 5:51 A.M., he lifted off from Folkestone, England, and set a course for France. Allen kept the craft steady, eight to ten feet above the water. After about an hour, the plane suddenly encountered rough air, and it quickly dropped close to the water. The waves of the Channel lapped at the fuselage, and Allen had trouble with the headwinds. Even worse, he felt his strength quickly draining from his body. It was no use, and he decided to ditch the plane into the sea. Using his last bit of energy, he pedaled furiously to get some height so that a boat could get underneath the aircraft. Miraculously, at fifteen feet, the air was much smoother. Soon his strength returned, and he decided to keep pedaling.

Slowly but surely, the Gossamer Albatross crossed the English Channel at speeds up to fifteen miles per hour. During the flight, the height and speed indicators stopped working, and the cockpit covering fogged up. Allen's calves and thighs cramped, and he ran out of water. The final test was flying over the offshore rocks before landing on the beach. Exhausted and in pain, Allen thought of crashing into them, but he managed to fly above the jagged barrier. At last he stopped pedaling, and the seventy-pound aircraft landed gently on the sands of France. The flight of the Gossamer Albatross had taken 2 hours and 49 minutes and had won MacCready's team the prize of about $300,000.

I came away from my meeting with the Rutans all excited about the prize idea for the NASP program. Unfortunately, I ran into a brick wall when I tested it on the government in Washington, D.C. "There are no provisions for such a procurement in the federal government," they said, and no one would even consider using a prize to motivate the American aerospace industry. Burt and Dick tried to sell the concept, but they also ran into insurmountable opposition. Every once in a while, we give it another try, but I don't think that we will ever be successful in getting the government to offer such a prize. Some breakthroughs have to wait for their time. But it may not matter. While the bureaucracy continues to debate that idea, we keep on making technical progress on the nearer-term commitment: developing an aerospace plane.

Karen's Little Song

On our oldest daughter's fifth birthday, my wife's parents sent us some money to buy a piano. They knew that we really couldn't afford to buy one, and they wanted their granddaughter to have the opportunity to play a musical instrument. No one of my side of the family has any musical talent, but my wife's dad has some natural, but undeveloped, musical capabilities. Since the bequest was very specific, my wife took Karen to the local piano and organ store with the intention of purchasing a modest piano. When they came back that evening, I found out that I would have to come up with some additional cash since the salesman had convinced them that a more expensive organ was a much better investment for our daughter. After squaring it with the grandparents, the sale was finalized, and the organ was delivered the next day.

One of the first problems we encountered was the relative sizes of Karen and the organ. If she sat on the organ bench, she could reach the keyboard, but she couldn't touch the foot pedals. If she stood up, the reverse was true. I was about to go strangle the fast-talking salesman when Karen came up with an innovative solution. She moved one of her play chairs to the organ, and by sitting on the front edge of the chair, she could work all the aspects of the organ. The salesman's life was spared, and we enrolled Karen in a beginner's class for piano and organ. I readied myself for what was sure to come—hours of monotonous plunking and the occasional chopsticks.

It wasn't like that at all. Karen had a terrific talent for the organ. Within weeks she was playing entire songs; not very complicated ones, but she rarely made a mistake. Her teacher recognized her capabilities and scheduled her with a more advanced instructor who specialized in young children. Her progress was phenomenal, and by the time she was six, she was playing complex songs which required a much more advanced organ. Since we couldn't afford a better organ, most of her practice time was spent at the piano and organ store, where she could use their larger organs.

Her first public performance was at a talent show sponsored by the store. Since I hadn't heard her practice the number that she would play, I was very anxious to attend the talent show. Several adults and older kids preceded her, and I was really beginning to feel nervous. These people were terrific; why in the world would they make her follow these semi-pros? The last guy sure looked like the fellow who played the pipe organ at the Cincinnati Reds Riverfront Stadium. It just wasn't fair to my little Karen.

When Karen came out in her fanciest dress and her new shoes with the required tape on the soles, everyone smiled. I know she's my daughter, but she really was the cutest thing. I assumed that they would wheel out a little organ for her to play. Instead, they brought out a little chair to replace the bench that was in front of the biggest organ that I had ever seen. There were three ascending keyboards on the organ, dozens of registration stops, and twenty-four foot pedals. With the little chair, she was able to reach two of the keyboards and half of the pedals. That was enough for her to perform a flawless rendition of "Ramblin Rose." There she was, completely dwarfed by the instrument, fingers darting across the keyboards and her little legs moving a mile a minute across the pedals. She really did a terrific job, and the crowd gave her a standing ovation. My wife and I were as proud as peacocks and more than a little overwhelmed when the owner asked if he could hire Karen to demonstrate organs in the store. We talked it over with Karen and accepted the offer on the condition that it didn't interfere with her school hours and bedtime schedule.

So, at six, Karen became a professional musician. For the next year, Karen got better and better. She practiced while she worked at the store, and the songs got much more difficult. There were more talent shows, and when she turned seven, she was entered in a regional contest sponsored by a major organ manufacturer. She won her age division and was automatically entered in the national competition in Philadelphia. The regional prize was a beautiful medal and an expense-paid trip for her and her family to the national competition. Three months later, Karen, Kristen, and Kim were packed into the back seat of the car, and off we went to Philadelphia.

The national contest was quite an event. Hundreds of kids from all over the nation were there. Although she was in the junior division, she was by far the smallest competitor at the event. The organs seemed even bigger than the ones at the store, and Karen had to be lifted onto the benches for her two mandatory performances. The first was a selection of her choosing—she played a well-practiced "Flight of the Bumble Bee" and received some very high scores from the judges.

The second was a complete surprise, something totally unanticipated. She was given a sequence of four random notes and allowed ten minutes to compose a song using those notes. Her eyes began to water when she was handed the notes, and my first reaction was to pull her out of this ridiculous contest. But she wouldn't let me do it. Instead, she took the sheet of paper and walked back to the corner of the room. As she sat there, I could see her little fingers jumping up and down, as she mentally composed the tune in her head. Ten minutes later, she got back on the stool and played a wonderful little song based on those four random notes. All of us were amazed at what she was able to create, and I've never been prouder of any of her musical performances. The judges really liked her creation, but her scores were not high enough for her to win the competition. When she finally was allowed to join us, we told her that she was terrific and that she really was the best, even if she didn't win. She looked up, gave us a big smile, and told us how scared she was when she was asked to compose her little song. "But," she said, "I wanted to do the song for you. So I did it in my head, and my fingers played the right notes."

Karen kept playing the organ and working at the store until she was about sixteen. After that, other priorities got in the way, and she now only plays for her own enjoyment (and that of her new husband). But every once in a while, on the very same organ that she started with, she'll whip out a few tunes. And somewhere in those brief performances, one song will catch my ear—her very own creation, the little song with those four familiar notes.

NASP Pioneers

The idea of building an aircraft that would fly into space has probably been around since man learned to fly. Even the 19th century balloonists were fascinated with going higher and higher, and if they could have made it to space, they would have tried. When the airplane came along, speed and altitude were limiting parameters, and it wasn't until the 1960s that the concept received any serious attention. There are historical documents which indicate that airbreathing propulsion was seriously considered as an alternative to rocket engines when the United States launched its major drive in space delivery systems in the 1950s. For a number of reasons, the rocketeers prevailed, and every space launch system from the early Atlas series through the Saturns to the Space Shuttle has used rocket propulsion. Since rockets have enormous thrust and do not require the outside air for propulsion, airplanes were ignored as an approach to get to space. Even in the 70s and early 80s, the dearth of work in advanced airbreathing propulsion and the inertia created by many successful rocket launches resulted in an absence of interest in aerospace planes.

In 1984, Tony duPont, one of the Delaware duPont's that had ventured into the aeronautical field, seriously began to consider the feasibility of an aerospace plane. Tony duPont had a very small and shaky aircraft and engine design company in San Diego, but he had been in the business for many years, and he was well-connected in Washington technical circles. After surveying the rapidly advancing state-of-the-art technology in materials, engines, and computational techniques, he concluded that things had progressed far enough that an aerospace plane might be feasible. Using a relatively simple computer program, Tony began inputting the available data and using the information to conceptually design an aerospace plane. Besides being very intelligent, Tony is also very entrepreneurial and optimistic. The more he played with his computer, the more excited he got about the possibility of an aerospace plane. After a while, he got so excited that he just had to tell someone about his work. So he decided to tell his friend, Bob Williams, about the results of his computer analysis.

While Tony was studying the feasibility of the aerospace plane in California, Bob Williams was just finishing up a project on advanced technology development in the Defense Advanced Research Projects Agency (DARPA) in Washington, D.C. Bob was a young visionary and very eager government scientist who had come to DARPA from the Navy several years earlier. As it is today, DARPA is a wonderful place to work if you want to light some fires in the technical world. Its staff numbers only around 100 people, and its budget is now in the billions. Favored by Congress because of its ability to act quickly and supportively, its mission is to start promising new technical projects which may have a large impact on future Department of Defense (DoD) systems. Over the years, DARPA has favored projects which are riskier than those that would be initiated by the DoD services themselves. The justification for this is that the high-risk projects also have the highest payoff. Fortunately for DARPA, the DoD services usually have to complete the projects started by DARPA. This has obviously led to some friction between DARPA and the services, particularly when the services have been stuck with a DARPA project that ended up in failure. Nevertheless, DARPA fills an important role, and its staff is usually populated with entrepreneurial civil servants who have strong personal missions in a particular technical area. Bob Williams fit all of those qualifications in spades, and he just happened to be looking for a mission in aeronautics when Tony duPont gave him a call.

The Bob Williams/Tony duPont connection was a marriage made in technology heaven, and they soon created a darling little aerospace plane. After introducing him to the concept, Tony kept Bob abreast of his design progress almost on a daily basis. Many long telephone conversations took place between these two as Tony reconfigured his airplane design to achieve higher and higher speeds, with the ultimate goal of Mach 25. One night, as Tony was working late on the West Coast, he called Bob to let him know that he was very close to the goal. They stayed on the phone until Tony redesigned the plane. In the early dawn hours of Washington, D.C., Bob heard Tony shout with joy as the computer generated an airplane that flew into space. It was like a spiritual experience, and the two became disciples for NASP from that point on. Several years later, Bob told me that he felt his mission with NASP was inspired from heaven. I have no doubt that he honestly felt that way.

Using Tony's technical savvy and Bob's clever persuasion, the duo launched an all-out attack on Washington, D.C. One by one, they conquered the pockets of resistance, turned enemies into allies, and transformed their supporters into zealots. A more in-depth feasibility study was quickly funded by Bob using DARPA resources. Simple technology demonstrations were defined and staged in front of prospective supporters in order to secure their commitment and generate stronger advocacy for the program. Bob Williams had the foresight to recognize that the development of an aerospace plane would require vast resources and very broad in-volvement. That would take some doing, but he was prepared to go to any length to get the aerospace plane off the ground.

One by one, their supporters grew. When some important person needed to be assured of the technical feasibility of the concept, Tony would be turned loose, and the prospective advocate would be shown some exciting technology demonstration. General Larry Skantze, head of the Air Force Systems Command, became a believer after he saw a spectacular engine demonstration and threw in his financial and political support. Ray Colladay, Associate Administrator at NASA, also joined the team and pledged to get NASA to join the parade. Scott Crossfield, former X-15 test pilot and later a congressional consultant, loved the idea and lent his legendary profile to NASP. It was very clear that the project was building up a head of steam, but Bob knew that he would need somebody very high up if he was going to succeed in transforming a paper concept into a major national program. The growing team targeted Dr. George Keyworth, President Reagan's science adviser in 1985, and they managed to get an audience in the White House. Since Keyworth has the combined characteristics of a Tony duPont and a Bob Williams, plus some, he loved the idea. As the program strategy was being developed by Williams, the big guns on the team laid out the political approach. Crossfield would line up some congressional support, Skantze and Colladay would kick in some money, DARPA would sponsor the program, and Keyworth would work on the president. In March of 1986, President Reagan delivered his State of the Union address to Congress. Tucked in the middle of his speech was the following sentence: "The United States will pursue the development of an airplane that will go from a runway on the ground to space. The Orient Express will also be able to take us around the world or to any place on the globe in less than two hours." While inaccurate in terms of its reference to an Orient Express (which has nothing to do with aerospace planes), the presidential statement officially launched the program and is still the basis on which the program rests today. When George Bush inherited the White House, he automatically supported the program that had been initiated by his friend and mentor, Ronald Reagan. Bob Williams, a lowly GS-14 at DARPA, and Tony duPont, a struggling aerospace engineer from California, had pulled off a major coup. Within several months of the early morning telephone call, they had transformed an idea into a presidential mandate.

But that was only the beginning. Now they needed a government infrastructure to manage the effort and an industrial team to implement the program. For six months, they worked twenty hours a day using every angle, every conceivable persuasion, and some well-placed threats to make it happen. When the smoke cleared, five government agencies had committed multi-year funding to the project. Even the Navy and the Strategic Defense Initiative office became partners in the deal. Despite the tremendous complexity of a five-agency joint program, Bob was able to convince the agencies' leadership of its merits.

American industry also was reluctant to jump on board such a scientifically shaky project. When technical arguments failed to convince a company's research and development managers, Bob would call the CEO and tell him that the president wanted his company on the program. The NASP program went under contract several months later, and every major aerospace company in America was a part of the team. Bob had done such a good job that all of the companies were also contributing significant money of their own to the program. To those of us in the aerospace field, NASP literally exploded onto the scene, and we were all swept up in its excitement and promise. Very few people understood how shallow the foundation of this program really was. It was a brilliant advocacy job by two very committed people who would not take no for an answer. With some modifications to the program, NASP is now on much firmer ground. But it would never have gotten started without the strong commitment of Tony duPont and Bob Williams.

Bob Williams ran the program from DARPA until 1987. He worked as hard during those two years as he did during the selling phase in 1985. He relentlessly lobbied the administration and Congress to financially support the program while he was involved in every detail of the contractor and government technical efforts. At one point in the budget debates in 1987, he became convinced that he needed the support of a key senator on the DoD Appropriations Committee. His normal procedure would have been to call Keyworth and ask him to intercede on NASP's behalf. Because of some unusual circumstances, he was forced to write a note to the White House asking for political support for the program. Unfortunately, this note somehow ended up in the secretary of defense's in-basket. The note was hand-written, irrefutably proving that Bob Williams, five management layers down from the secretary of defense, was going around the "system" and attempting to influence the president on a DoD program matter. Bob Williams was fired the next day, and his involvement in the program ceased abruptly. I see him every now and then, and there is no bitterness in his memory. He's just glad that he was able to start the ball rolling.

Tony duPont continued to work on his computer program and never did integrate well into the national industry team that took on NASP. Despite many attempts by a lot of people on his behalf, he maintained a somewhat adversarial technical relationship with the team that he and Bob had created. Nevertheless, he is widely regarded as the father of NASP and is appropriately recognized as the spark which lit the fire.

Principles

In the final analysis, the key to creativity is commitment. Major change will be rejected by most organizations until it is the last, and perhaps only remaining, alternative. All we have to do is look at ourselves to prove the point. The human organism is designed to attack any intruder that is attempting to change the status quo. If a foreign virus or bacteria enters our system, millions of antibodies are released to destroy the outsider before it can take hold. Only if the virus defeats the army of defenders will it be successful in changing our system. That's why habits are so hard to break. Once we become stable in the habit, our bodies will fight the change, even when it's in our eventual best interest. Organizations are made up of people, and they react to change in the same way.

It takes tremendous amounts of determination and persistence to make major changes in an organization. The bureaucracy will fight change, the establishment will fight change, and the system will fight change. The only way to succeed is to fight back with all of your strength, wit, and power. That can only be done if you are totally committed to the cause. Since breakthroughs are enormous changes, it will take enormous commitment to make them happen. The barriers will be very high, and breaking through them is analogous to a single molecule of hydrogen penetrating a one-foot plate of aluminum. But that does happen, as we have actually experienced on the NASP program. Extraordinary commitment can penetrate the strongest resistance, and commitment is a very personal decision.

Every one of us has certain values and principles that we will not compromise. Some of us have more values than others and some of the principles are more noble than others. But each of us has at least one that we will fight for, maybe even to the death. I really don't have many that fit into that category, but I do have one minor cause to which I am totally committed. It's silly, but I absolutely refuse to let the transportation systems in America get the best of me. When I've decided to go to some place on some date, I go through all sorts of antics to make sure I get there when I want to. I guess I should just use a good travel agent, but I just love to attack this system myself. I'm a frequent flyer on almost every airline, and a frequent renter at all the major car rental agencies, so I work the system until I get what I want. At the risk of getting into trouble, I double-book and do whatever it takes to get what I want. It's such a small and stupid thing, but I feel so good when I successfully get to my destination at minimum cost and in minimum time. Over the past five years, I've traveled half a million miles, and I really can't recall a single trip that was a disaster. Maybe I should become a travel agent. My point, though, is that commitment can get you over all kinds of obstacles. Once you really decide to make it happen, it really will happen.

Victory belongs to the most persevering.

—Napoleon

---

commitment
determination
persistence,

CHAPTER 7

Organized Adventure
The Journey

Oh, I have slipped the surly bonds of earth
And danced the skies on laughter-silvered wings;
Sunward I've climbed, and joined the tumbling mirth
Of sun-split clouds—and done a hundred things
You have not dreamed of—wheeled and soared and swung
High in the sunlit silence. Hov'ring there,
I've chased the shouting wind along, and flung
My eager craft through footless halls of air
Up, up the long, delirious, burning blue
I've topped the windswept heights with easy grace
Where never lark, or even eagle flew
And, while with silent, lifting mind I've trod
The high untrespassed sanctity of space
Put out my hand, and touched the face of God.
—High Flight by John Gillespie Magee, Jr.

Our adventures are the highlights of our lives, at least that's how we tell it around the office water cooler. We lay out four thousand bucks for a romantic seven-day Caribbean vacation and then spend all of our time talking about the twenty-five-dollar, ten-minute para-sailing experience that we foolishly let ourselves get talked into taking. We were scared to death, but wow, was it a wild ride. We'll never forget it for as long as we live.

We all seem drawn to adventure, at least occasionally, and if only in our minds. It's exciting, and it gets our juices flowing. We're forced into the unknown, and it challenges us to deal with circumstances that are foreign to our everyday lives. Some of the time, the adventure is thrust upon us, like emergencies or crises. Sometimes we are tempted or coerced into an adventure, like when your youngest son reminds you that any other parent would climb a tree to retrieve a snarled kite. And occasionally, we just go for it. Somewhere around the end of January, after religiously watching pro-football on TV for seventeen consecutive Sundays, we finally decide that we're going to learn how to snow ski. The fact that we've been inundated for four months by beer commercials that show downhill skiers getting all the beautiful women may have something to do with it. Nevertheless, we plunge into the adventure and, if we survive, it becomes the greatest thing in our lives, at least until we get bored again and another adventure takes its place.

Adventures do bring out the best in most people. They force us to deal with complexity and challenge, and survival or success requires the best that we can muster. Since we are being confronted with unfamiliar circumstances, they also elicit creativity and innovation. They are the perfect setting for breakthroughs, so why not set ourselves up for success—organize the adventure.

Kelly Johnson

In 1985, the Air Force and the Navy initiated a project called Forecast II. It was an attempt to predict the future direction of military aeronautics by examining the past progress in this area, the present state of the art, and the possible futures that could be envisioned. As the name implies, there had been an earlier effort, known simply as Project Forecast, that had been conducted in the 60s. A very successful program, it laid the foundation for the development of ballistic missiles, stealth aircraft, and military space satellites. Because of the success of Project Forecast, the military leadership felt confident that the results of Forecast II would be very valuable in charting the future course for the aerospace community. Forecast II did yield some interesting predictions when it was over, but perhaps its most valuable contribution was its revelations about the past. One of the earliest outputs of the project was a comparative study of aircraft development over the past thirty years. One comparison was particularly noteworthy and really tells the whole story.

Towards the end of the 50s, two major aircraft programs were initiated, one to build a high-altitude, high-speed reconnaissance aircraft and the other to build a high-performance, highly maneuverable fighter aircraft. The reconnaissance aircraft program was stimulated by the national concern with the activities that were occurring in the Soviet Union. The objective was to develop a plane that would fly so high and so fast that it would be invulnerable to any ground or airborne defense system. The task was given to the Lockheed Corporation's Advanced Development Division and the project was initiated in September 1958. Within six months, the Skunk Works, as the division was known, had completed the preliminary design of an airplane that would be capable of achieving speeds of Mach 3+ (about 2,000 miles per hour) and flying at altitudes above 80,000 feet. After the go-ahead from the government, it took the Skunk Works only twelve months to build the aircraft, and the first flight of the Mach 3 airplane occurred in 1962. Made out of black titanium metal so that the structure could withstand the high temperature of Mach 3 flight, the aircraft was labelled the Blackbird. It completed its flight testing in six months, became operational in 1964, and the fleet of Blackbirds flew hundreds of missions until all the aircraft were retired in 1991. Luckily, several of the retired Blackbirds were picked up by NASA for flight testing at Edwards Air Force Base, and two of the aircraft are still operational today, as research airplanes. I was lucky enough to fly in the last trainer Blackbird in 1992 and feel what it's really like to go Mach 3.2. FAST!!! When the records of the Blackbird project were finally released, they revealed that the development of this airplane was accomplished in less than twenty-seven months and that the Blackbird Skunk Works Team led by Kelly Johnson numbered only several hundred people. The estimated cost of the development effort was several hundred million dollars.

By contrast, the fighter aircraft program, started about the same time as the Blackbird program, resulted in the highly effective

F-15 aircraft that is produced by the McDonnell Douglas Aircraft Corporation. Generally acknowledged as today's foremost fighter airplane, the F-15 is a highly maneuverable, extremely versatile weapon system that can achieve speeds in excess of Mach 2. The F-15 became operational in 1982 and is currently still in the Air Force inventory, although the versatile F-16, the stealthy F-17, and the operational F-22 will eventually limit its use. The development of the F-15 took over 20 years and involved the talents of over 180,000 aerospace employees in several dozen companies. The development cost of the F-15 has been estimated at $20 billion.

While it's not fair to directly compare the development efforts of the Blackbird and the F-15, the Forecast II team was struck by the tremendous difference between the cost and time required for each effort. How could the world's fastest military aircraft be built in less than three years when typical development times for sophisticated airplanes were generally fifteen to twenty years? How could several hundred people produce an incredibly capable reconnaissance vehicle when most current aircraft programs require tens of thousands of individuals? Since project costs are generally a function of project duration and personnel levels, could small, fast teams be the solution to the escalating cost requirements of military aircraft? What happened during the development of the Blackbird that allowed this breakthrough system to mature in such a short time, with so few resources, with such a small team? The answer, it seems, was Kelly Johnson, and the way he ran the Lockheed Skunk Works.

Kelly Johnson approached his assignments in a unique way. He had fourteen rules that governed the way he conducted business with the government. Paraphrased, they are:

1. Managers must be delegated complete control of their programs.

2. Project offices must be strong and small.

3. The number of people must be restricted in an almost vicious manner.

4. Very simple systems must be used.

5. There must be a minimum number of reports.

6. Never surprise the customer.

7. Responsibility must be delegated.

8. Never pay for something that doesn't work.

9. Test the final product in flight.

10. Thoroughly understand the goal before you begin.

11. Pay people promptly.

12. There must be mutual trust.

13. Access by outsiders must be strictly controlled.

14. Good performance, and not rank, must be rewarded.

While all of Kelly's rules make perfectly good sense and are really the foundation for structured flexibility and competitive collaboration, his last unstated rule made all the difference between the Skunk Works operation and those of his aerospace competitors. In several interviews that took place after he retired, Kelly Johnson revealed that he had one tenet which underpinned everything that transpired at the Skunk Works. He said that he decided early on that he would only work on adventures and that every project he accepted would be an adventure. He carefully chose the projects that the Skunk Works would go after, declared them an adventure, and carried them out in an adventurous fashion. Even the nickname Skunk Works added to the mystique. Everyone thought Kelly was conjuring up some magic brews in the off-limits aircraft production facility, so they compared it to the Skunk Works moonshine still in the Li'l Abner cartoon. Because it was an adventure, everyone was excited, and everyone gave the project their very best efforts. Because of this, progress could be made by a very small team, and breakthroughs like the Blackbird could be achieved. Organizing each project as an adventure not only helped in the production of breakthrough aircraft, it also resulted in the production of adventures.

The St. Helen Festival

Once a year, starting in January and lasting until the first weekend in June, my home becomes a storage house for hundreds of stuffed animals, well-dressed Barbie dolls, and paperback books. As the items accumulate, the garage becomes overloaded, and any place in the house is fair game. It's not unusual to open a closet and have a six-foot Panda jump on your head. The only saving grace is that we are not involved with the raffle booths that give away goldfish or plants as prizes. I don't think that I would be able to take a bath with those little fishes swimming around me or take a shower with ivy growing up my leg.

The focal point for all this activity is the annual St. Helen Festival, the largest outdoor church festival in Ohio. Last year, despite some rain, the festival made over $200,000 during a two-day period. More than 2,000 parishioners were involved in putting on the event, and that rivaled the attendance at all masses on Sundays. Tens of thousands of people attended the festival, which culminated with a drawing for the grand prize (originally a house, now $10,000). The profit from the festival is integrated with the weekly collections and provides a welcome reserve for the pastor to use as repairs and upgrades are needed in the school. While the parish could financially survive without the festival, this was not always the case. Besides, everybody would want to have the festival even if it didn't make a penny.

The parish was formed about thirty-five years ago, and it serves about 7,000 people. The old timers tell us that the first building on the parish grounds was a small elementary school. The church came later. The founders felt that an elementary school for the children was more critical than a church, so they built that first, primarily through volunteer help and contributions. They used the school for the lower elementary grades, and they set aside space in one of the rooms for masses on Sundays. It soon became obvious that they needed more classrooms, and what's a parish without a church. The dilemma, as usual, was money. It was not an affluent parish, and it was obvious that some, if not most, of the money to expand the school and build the church would have to come from outside of the parish. Being a resourceful group, they decided to raise money for the parish through an annual festival. We Catholics seem to accept modest gambling and good-hearted beer drinking when the cause is right. So, naturally, the festival included its share of raffles, wheels of fortune, and, of course, bingo. There was also a beer booth, which later became a beer garden, and lots of food, games, and rides.

The festival began in a modest fashion, with one or two rides and several food booths and games of chance. By the time I joined the parish in 1972, the St. Helen Festival had become a major operation with over 50 booths, a good-size carnival section, several beer trucks, and over 1,000 volunteer workers. To my amazement, the two-day festival, which was always held on the first weekend in June, netted over $100,000 and was contributing about one-third of the parish revenues for the entire year. What started off as a supplementary fundraiser had turned into the major social and resource event of the year, every year. Calendars and other church events were organized around the festival, and everyone in the parish, if not the city, anxiously awaited the June event.

In the world of aerospace planes, $100,000 is not a gigantic sum. But for a small Catholic parish, it's big bucks. When I found out what this festival made, I just had to find out how they did it. It took me several years, lots of volunteer time, and I finally got roped into serving as the general chairman of the festival, but I did find out. It was the most organized adventure I had ever run across. Not only did it make lots of money and intensely involve almost everyone in the parish, but everybody loved it.

As soon as a festival ended, they started planning the next one. While the volunteer accounting staff was adding up the tally and paying the bills, the previous co-chairman organized the activities for the following twelve months. Prizes for the next June's festival were ordered in September, people's vacation schedules for next summer were planned around the festival, and the booth chairmen began gathering their workers in December. Every July there was a victory party, and the people who sold the most raffle tickets were honored and encouraged to do even better next year. By January, the activity was really revving up. Tiny clothes for the doll raffle booth were being made in almost every household. The general ticket chairman organized the entire parish into ticket districts, and every family was given their fair share to sell. I remember my three girls rushing to the neighbors' houses as soon as we got our tickets so that they could beat the other Catholic kids to the punch. The big incentive for the youngsters was the reward for selling two books of tickets. If they did, they would be excused from wearing the mandatory school uniform for one week in the spring. While those simple, interchangeable uniforms were our salvation many a morning in my home, my three daughters naturally wanted some variety. Being able to wear jeans for a week provided all the motivation that the grade school kids needed.

By April, the festival activity was at a fever pitch. Over 200 chairmen and managers were needed to pull off the weekend event in an organized fashion. A carnival company was hired to provide and run the rides, and it was always fun dealing with those gypsies. Fifty auxiliary police were "rented" for the festival so that no trouble would mar the event. Three weeks before the festival weekend, construction of the tents, booths, and rides began. Almost every man in the parish showed up for at least one evening of construction. The schoolyard became a circus, and volunteer electricians would lay miles of cable and wires for the lighting and sound crews. Around 8:30 every evening, the old pastor would come out with a few six-packs of beer to thank the guys for their help. There were always barrels of ice and pop to give to the kids who were willing to help.

When Festival Friday finally arrived, all of the workers would attend a church service to pray for a successful event. After that, people would work until they dropped. We always stayed well past midnight, went home for a few hours of sleep, and came back early the next day. It was the best time of the year, the happiest weekend, and everybody helped each other in any way they could. If it rained, and invariably we would have a typical Dayton summer shower sometime during the weekend, people would not leave their posts, serving food or drinks in the pouring rain, so as not to encourage the crowd to leave. I have seen grown men and women cry because of a prolonged shower, fearing that it would seriously hurt the parish's major revenue source. When it did rain, Father would come around and tell everyone not to worry, that it was just God's way. Amazingly, it usually stopped raining after he made his rounds.

By Sunday night, when the grand prize was drawn, everyone was exhausted. People went around hugging each other, congratulating everyone on their successes, and making notes for next year's improvements. That was the one moment during the year when the parish was really a living, loving community. Politics, animosities, and differences were all put aside, and the true nature of Christian fellowship came out. Every year, the same thing happened. It was wonderful, and it was extraordinary. At 5 P.M. on the following day, a kickoff meeting was held in the church basement to organize the next festival adventure.

Passing the Chuck

Outward Bound experiences are terrific ways to build team spirit. But they all involve some great personal challenges. It was obvious to everyone on one particular Outward Bound experience I attended that the big challenge was going to be Chuck. Chuck weighs about 270 pounds and wears a size 50 belt. Since most of us were engineers, we knew that these two parameters were critical in determining our plan of attack. There were about fifteen spaces in the simulated rope spider web that had been strung up between the two trees by our instructor. Only one of them looked big enough to accommodate Chuck. Unfortunately, it was about four feet from the ground.

The nine of us were trying to figure out a strategy that would meet the fourth challenge of this cold November morning. We had already built a bridge across the creek, climbed some poles, and tightrope walked across a small ravine. So far, we hadn't lost anybody, and everyone was in great spirits. We hadn't counted on the cold when we had planned this outing. But you never know what to expect in the Midwest in November. Most of us had brought some extra clothing, so we weren't really uncomfortable. It just would have been so much more pleasant if the sun had been shining. And besides, the two sweaters that he had put on expanded Chuck's cross-section by at least two more inches. How would we solve "The Chuck Problem"?

At first we tried to convince Chuck to make a flying leap through the large hole. If he was successful and the tiny bell hanging from one of the strings didn't ring, the rest of us would work our way to the other side using different holes. I've got to give him credit; he was about to give it a try when we stopped him. The probability of him even jumping that high was pretty small, let alone getting through the hole without ringing the bell. And would he survive hitting the ground or the trees? Would the trees survive? So we stopped him and came up with a new plan. Since the rules only allowed one person to use any specific hole, we each picked a hole that we thought would accommodate our size, reserving the big one for Chuck. Some of the spaces were pretty high, so it was obvious that some lifting was going to be required. In addition, some of us would have to get on the other side early so that we could catch the high divers and break their fall.

Being the smallest, I went first and dove through the small hole about halfway up the web. I rang the bell and had to try it again. Fortunately, I was the first; otherwise everyone would have been required to start over when the bell rang. My second try was successful. Two more people came across without ringing the bell. We still needed one more to cross before we would attempt passing "The Chuck." The fourth guy, the second largest of the group, actually hit the bell. We tried to argue about the rules, but the instructor sent us all back to the other side. Ten minutes later, the four of us had made it through to the other side.

Chuck was then asked to lay on the ground with his legs crossed and his arms extended down his sides. The four people in front of the web, three men and a woman, were to lift him up as if he were levitating. The plan was to pass Chuck through the hole in a way that was similar to threading a needle. The four of us on the other side would receive him in a like fashion, guide his feet, then his legs, and finally his upper body through the hole, and then lower him to the ground. Three more people would then attempt their holes with some help from both sides. And the last person, the most athletic in the group, would dive through, landing in the arms of the eight receivers. The four lifters took a deep breath, dug in their heels, and slowly raised Chuck to the height of the hole. He was as stiff as a board, and it looked like our strategy was going to work. His feet came through, then his legs, and we were about to push even further. That's when we realized that he would definitely hit the string and jingle the bell. That hole was the biggest one in the web, but it was not big enough for Chuck. We again lodged a formal protest, but the instructor turned a deaf ear. Now what?

Chuck was moved backwards and lowered to the ground as we contemplated our dilemma. We needed some creative thinking, but no one was able to come up with a solution. Trying to modify the rules got us nowhere; every objection was overruled by the evil instructor. As we were debating, Chuck moved out of his corpse-like position, stood up, and started removing his clothes. Layer by layer, Chuck began to get smaller and smaller. When he got down to his shorts, he stopped, laid down on the ground, and asked everyone to try again. He must have been terribly cold (it was about 40° Fahrenheit), but he never complained. The four lifted him up and began to pass him through. Just before we got to his midpoint, he sucked in his breath as hard as he could, and we gingerly moved him past the strings, one millimeter at a time. Success, but just by the hair of his chinny-chin-chin. Tremendous cheering erupted, even though the other four still had to make it through. We passed Chuck's clothes through, one piece at a time, and he got dressed again so that he could help us with the remaining people.

As luck would have it, the seventh person rang the bell, and we had to do it all over again. More diving, more catching, Chuck did his striptease, and with some more belly-sucking, we got him through again. When the last person came through, we all jumped on Chuck, partly to give him some warmth and partly to get as close as we could to each other. We had made it, we had beaten the spider, and there was nothing that could stop us now. We spent the rest of the day climbing trees, screaming like eagles, and scaling a twenty-foot vertical wall using only tiny crevices as hand and foot holds. About 5 P.M., we came back to the lodge and ate like there was no tomorrow. Most of us were totally exhausted, and everyone was asleep by 8 P.M.

The next morning, we reviewed the happenings of the previous day and concluded that we had done some pretty amazing things. Besides being able to pass Chuck through the hole, almost every person had accomplished something individually that they never thought was possible. Many had experienced a miniature personal breakthrough, and there were some team accomplishments that we also considered pretty incredible. Just before we climbed onto the bus to return home to Dayton, we took a group picture with Chuck in his shorts.

It had been a great adventure, one that we would recall many times as we worked together on the aerospace plane. We had formed some strong bonds during that adventure. More importantly, the experience taught us that we could do some unbelievable things if we had the right attitude. We've tried to maintain that spirit of adventure as we've tackled some very different kinds of challenges. As the bus passed the two trees tied together with the spider web, we all smiled. How in the world were we able to pass Chuck through that tiny hole?

The Sky Is No Longer the Limit

The burial of Stu Schmidt was a memorable experience for me. After the last eulogy was read, Ted went over to the coffin to place one red rose on Stu's chest. He grabbed the lid of the coffin and slowly began to lower it over the body of Captain Stu Schmidt, U.S. Navy. "Like hell," cried Stu, "I'm getting out of here." Of course, he couldn't. At least not under his own power. To make it tolerable for him to lay in a coffin for three hours while all of his friends, dressed in black, paid their respects, a special rig had been constructed which fed vodka and tonic into Stu's mouth whenever he wanted some. Stu was drunk, almost dead drunk, and he could barely lift his head, let alone his body, out of the coffin. Several of the guys helped him out, propped him in a chair, and the party continued until late into the night.

The occasion of Stu Schmidt's burial was prompted by his firing from the NASP program and his subsequent quick retirement from the Navy. It was the first time I had to fire one of my friends, but the order came down from General Bernie Randolph, Commander of the Air Force Systems Command, and I had no recourse. For several days, I had tried to calm the storm that erupted after Stu had written the note criticizing the Air Force for backing out of a facilities deal for NASP. But the note had reached the big guys in Washington, and they were determined to make Stu an example. NASP has always been a highly political program, where perceptions are sometimes more important than reality. A breach of faith between two services in a joint-service program causes a real flap in Washington. When that breach is broadcast via a written note, it leads to all kinds of embarrassment. Usually, someone's head has to roll. In this case, they decided to shoot the messenger. Stu didn't help his case by editorializing in the note and continuing to protest. In the end, I was directed to tell Stu that he had to leave the program, and Stu decided it was a fine time to retire from the Navy. So, naturally, we decided to have a celebration, and a wake seemed very appropriate at the time.

From the start of the program in 1985 to this day, that's the way it's been in the NASP program—one giant crazy adventure. A recent article about the NASP program stated that it began in turmoil, and it's been tumultuous ever since. That's true, and the chaos and excitement have been as invigorating as they have been stressful. They have forced everyone in the program to operate flat-out, and living on the edge has stimulated some incredible creativity and innovation.

While Bob Williams and Tony duPont were selling the NASP program in Washington, some of us at Wright-Patterson Air Force Base were trying to determine the best technical direction for aerospace planes. We had organized about thirty of our best engineers and scientists into a three-month study team to examine the state of the art of aerospace technology, as well as the potential of an aerospace plane. They concluded that an airplane which would be capable of achieving Mach 25 was not feasible. Rather, the technology growth that they projected over the next ten years would only allow the development of aircraft in the Mach 6–8 range. In the meantime, Williams and duPont continued to advocate the Mach 25 aerospace plane.

One of the more innovative directors at Wright-Patterson decided to test the foundation of the thirty-man study team report. He asked a dozen of the team members if they would be willing to re-examine the issue, under slightly different conditions. They agreed, and he rented a nearby seminarian retreat house for two weeks. When the twelve engineers showed up on the first day of the off-site, they found themselves joined by several nationally prominent science-fiction writers. The heterogeneous team struggled with the issue for the two-week period and came to a somewhat different conclusion than the original group. They concluded that the technology might soon exist to allow airplanes to reach Mach numbers in the 12–14 regime and that a two-plane (one on top of the other) system might just make it to Mach 25. In the meantime, Williams and duPont continued to advocate the Mach 25 aerospace plane.

I was fascinated by the results of the "retreat house" team and began to wonder just how much influence the science-fiction writers had on the more optimistic results. Just for the fun of it, I asked several of the engineers who had been on both teams to indulge me in yet a third review of aerospace technology. Without telling them what I was up to, I asked them to meet me at a nearby hotel, where I had rented a conference room for the day. After they had arrived, I marched in my mystery guests, four fifth-graders from my parish's elementary school. Being good sports, the engineers began to explain their tasking to the young students. As they talked, the kids warmed up to the topic and began asking lots of questions. "Why can't you build an airplane that flies in space?" asked a ten-year-old. "Because there's no air in space," replied the engineers. "Bring some with you," said the only little girl. "Hmm." (The fact that the current NASP concept collects, liquefies, and stores air as it moves through the atmosphere may just be coincidental, but who knows?) "Why can't you build an airplane instead of a rocket to go to space?" said the kids. "Because rockets carry lots of fuel and we can't get enough in an airplane to go to space," was the engineers' logical answer. "Make the airplane real big and stuff it full of thick fuel," said one of the little boys. "Hmm." (The fact that the current NASP concept has a seventy percent fuel fraction on takeoff and uses very dense slush hydrogen as a fuel may also be a coincidence, but who really knows?) And so it went, until the middle of the afternoon. By then, the kids were bored, and the engineers had concluded that there just might be a way to build an airplane that would make it to space. In the

Like schwandt said, go back to be little kids

meantime, Williams and duPont had sold the Mach 25 National Aero-Space Plane program.

And that's how the adventure began. Maybe because of this auspicious beginning, the program has attracted some of the most interesting and unique people in the aerospace community. Captured by a mission that was next to impossible, they have remained determined to reach the goal and to have a wonderful time along the way. There was so much optimism in the beginning that the program immediately attracted test pilots who wanted to fly the airplane. Not realizing that it would take more than a decade or so to get to flight testing, they volunteered for the program only to be given a desk to sit at in the Joint Program Office in Dayton, Ohio. Even Scott Crossfield, now seventy-two years old, thought that there might be a chance that he could fly the airplane. I keep telling him that we were moving as fast as we could, but I didn't think we would make it in time for him. Colonel Ted Wierzbanowski (W+12), test pilot on the X-29; Steve Ishmael, NASA test pilot; and Joe Engle, the astronaut, have been part of the program since the beginning. These people and all of their pals live for adventure, and, thank goodness, they have brought that element into the program.

About once a week, Ted would walk around the program office measuring the "energy level" of the group. Based purely on his subjective judgment, he would decide whether a party was in order. Almost invariably, he determined that it was. I will always remember the time when Ted stormed into my office carrying two giant turkeys, one in each hand. Even though it was June, Ted decided that it was Thanksgiving, and by the end of the day, everyone was outside feasting on the birds. Naturally, it was Ted who decided to give Stu a wake after he was fired. How he got the casket I'll never know, but his neighbors never could quite understand what was happening at his house almost every Saturday night. I remember the last party Ted threw before he left for California. It was a toga party and great fun, as long as you came in a toga. Anyone who didn't was actually crucified on the front lawn until they conformed. When they had agreed to change into a sheet, they were let down and joined the party. Amazingly, no one got upset. After all, we were living an adventure.

The other test pilots were constantly pushing to get something into the air as soon as possible. Unfortunately, the only complete airplanes that we have been able to fabricate were the mock-ups that were made by our student helpers. Even these productions have given the program a tremendous sense of excitement. After the great success with the first mock-up built by Virginia Tech, we initiated a national competition in 1991 to build a second mock-up with the new design. The senior mechanical engineering class at Mississippi State won the contest and delivered a fantastic mock-up to the second U.S. Air Show in 1992. The vice president saw the authentic-looking mock-up and asked if there was any way to fly the thing. Several organizations designed a second version of the mock-up, which could be dropped from an airplane and be capable of gliding to a landing. Although it would definitely have to be an unmanned flight, we've had all kinds of volunteers for the flight. To make their case, the test pilots convinced me to take a ride in the SR-71 Blackbird. Steve Ishmael took us up to Mach 3.2 and 85,000 feet, giving me the most exciting airborne experience of my life. Now I'm ready to fly the wooden mock-up to a landing.

While the test pilots have been more visible, the engineers and the managers on the program are also living an adventure. These folks have consistently pushed the state of the art in program management, business practices, and technology development. They have pioneered new ways of government-industrial cooperation, award-fee motivational processes, interservice cooperation, international relationships, program advocacy, and technical cooperation. These innovations have allowed the scientists and engineers in the program to break some barriers and probe new areas of technical possibilities. Many people have gone out on very long limbs to keep the program successful. Unfortunately, several have paid the price. Like Bob Williams and Stu Schmidt, many have sacrificed their careers for this program. Colonel Tom Bishop, a true friend of NASP, spent a long, lonely year at a remote northern Air Force base because of his relentless, and evidently embarrassing, support of the program. But he came right back to Washington and rejoined the team, just like nothing had ever happened. There were many more little adventures, and some that I still can't mention.

Several months ago, I was asked by a friend to give a dinner speech at the annual awards ceremony of his organization. Since he had heard one of my usual program talks on NASP, he asked if I could personalize my talk and discuss how it felt to be involved with NASP. As an incentive, he insisted on inviting my wife and three daughters to join us that evening at the head table. I spent a long time preparing for that speech, trying to decide what to say and what not to say about living on a roller coaster for six years. On the night of the event, I threw all my notes away and decided to wing it, regardless of the consequences. With the four most important women in my life and several hundred other people in front of me, I opened with a confession. I admitted to having a long, wonderful affair with one of the most exciting and beautiful ladies that I have ever seen. I paused for a moment, long enough to see eight flashing eyes and four very flushed faces. "Let me tell you about this lady," I said. "She's long and sleek and fast, and she's one hot number. She has kept me up many nights, but she has one of the most exhilarating bodies that I've ever seen. She keeps me on my toes, she's always unpredictable, and when you're with her, she can take you out of this world."

My family has finally forgiven me for putting them on the spot. Maybe I could have used a different approach to explain what the last six years have been like. Maybe, but how can you convey what it's like to live a great adventure? Besides, describing the adventure isn't the important thing. Living the adventure is what counts. And when you do, the sky is no longer the limit.

Principles

There is plenty of evidence to suggest that success can be achieved through hard work, clear objectives, unwavering commitment, and good teamwork. Breakthroughs also can result from the same behavior, but most breakthroughs have another ingredient. While it's impossible to describe this factor with one word, spirit comes the closest. It's a combination of excitement and energy, joy and pride, emotion and exhilaration, faith and confidence, and many other feelings. It's the noncerebral, intuitive, sensory, emotional, holistic part of the equation. While the brain may do most of the work, spirit brings in the heart and the soul, and most of the time, that makes a world of difference. But where does this spirit come from? And how can we bring it to the endeavor?

If we review the words that have been used to describe this breakthrough ingredient, we find that they also can be applied to other events in our lives. The first one that comes to mind is falling in love. Think about it—isn't "falling" in love a breakthrough? Another might be a strong spiritual event. While some projects may indeed involve romance or spirituality (it's amazing how many breakthrough stories did have spiritual or romantic elements), it's going to be difficult to base our breakthrough leadership efforts on getting people to fall in love or be born again.

A more appropriate and reasonable activity that also encompasses all of those characteristics is the adventure. Adventures capture our imagination, satisfy our souls, get the juices flowing, and heighten our senses. It's stressful, yet exciting; it opens up our world, and it often requires the commitment of our entire being. If we could make our activities into adventures, we could bring out all of these important characteristics. But we must be honest; we must really make them adventures. Just calling something an adventure won't hack it—these adventures have to push or pull us beyond our normal limits.

At any point in our career or our life, we can be either on a job or on a journey. Our jobs keep us going; our journeys take us places. Making the journey an adventure can lead us to some very exciting places. It may even lead us to a breakthrough.

Don't wait for your ship to come in,
swim out to it.

—Unknown

CHAPTER 8

Breakthrough Leadership
Six IDEAs

---

*There is one thing stronger
than all the armies of the world,
and that is an IDEA
whose time has come.*

—Victor Hugo

So far we have concentrated on what it takes to create breakthroughs, and we have seen that breakthroughs involve some, and often all, of the characteristics described in the last six chapters. But how do we develop these characteristics? If we want our teams to deliver breakthroughs, there's only one answer. As leaders, we must foster, encourage, and, in some cases, provide the characteristics that lead to breakthroughs. Specifically, breakthrough leaders must:

1. develop and communicate those captivating challenges that inspire breakthroughs,

2. create and maintain a sense of open focus that will lead to innovation,

135

3. encourage and motivate a spirit of collaboration within a highly competitive environment,

4. develop and foster both the structure and the flexibility needed for creativity,

5. inspire and stimulate broad personal commitment to the vision, and

6. lead the team on the organized adventure of the breakthrough.

As we've seen, these are the "whats" of breakthrough leadership—what the leader must do to maximize the probability of a breakthrough. How the leader does it will be very dependent on the personality and style of the leader.

Every leader, every person for that matter, has certain strengths and weaknesses. Even the best of leaders have their downsides and flaws, and all of them perform certain leadership functions better than others. If you look at the list of breakthrough leadership tasks outlined above, it's difficult to believe that anyone would be able to excel in all of the required areas. Some of us are pretty good at dealing with flexibility and chaos, but we drop the ball when it comes to providing the required structure and focus. Others can create a vision and a focused goal, but find it hard to inspire personal commitment or develop a sense of adventure. Usually, most leaders will go with their strengths in trying to create a climate for breakthroughs. That's reasonable, but it may definitely lessen the chances of achieving one. It may even defeat the purpose of the project or team by driving the group or group members too far in one direction. Ideally, the leader should strive to create all of the conditions that stimulate breakthroughs. But how? Well, I've collected a few ideas on the "hows" of breakthrough leadership. Six ideas, to be specific, one for each of the six needed characteristics. And to make the six ideas easy for me to remember, I've used something that is a mainstay in the government aerospace world, the acronym.

From the beginning, it was never the National Aero-Space Plane; it was always NASP. We never worked in the System Program Office;

we were in the SPO. If our project had been the World Aero-Space Plane, it would have been the WASP; worse, the Global Aero-Space Plane would have been GASP. In my earlier laser days, we called the Air Force Weapons Laboratory/Aero Propulsion Laboratory effort the AFWL APL (pronounced the awful apple). Keeping true to this crazy tradition, I offer a few IDEAs on the "hows" of breakthrough leadership. While they may seem a bit forced, they really represent tried and proven ways that breakthrough leaders have achieved success. Here are the six IDEAs:

The First **IDEA**—Creating Captivating Challenges

Tapping into the   Inventor

Dreamer

Explorer

Adventurer

The Second **IDEA**—Maintaining Open Focus

Leading through   Inspiring

Developing

Encouraging

Allowing

The Third **IDEA**—Synergizing Competitive Collaboration

Teaming the   Intuitive

Directed

Evaluative

Assertive

The Fourth **IDEA**—Developing Structured Flexibility

Fostering

Intrapreneuring

Diversity

Experimentation

"Adhocracy"

The Fifth **IDEA**—Nurturing Personal Commitment

Acting with

Integrity

Direction

Empowerment

Alignment

The Sixth **IDEA** — Producing Organized Adventure

Living with

Intensity

Determination

Enthusiasm

Abandon

The First IDEA—Creating Captivating Challenges

Tapping into the Inventor, Dreamer, Explorer, and Adventurer

My favorite training instrument is the Myers-Briggs Behavioral Style Inventory. If you've ever taken the Myers-Briggs test, you know that it examines your behavioral preferences and categorizes you in terms of how you deal with the world, what you pay attention to, how you make decisions, and how structured you are. Depending on how you answer the questions on the test, you receive one of sixteen four-letter indicators (I'm an ENFP) that can be related to your leadership and managerial styles. The four-letter Myers-Briggs indicator reveals a great deal about your management characteristics, but I'm always fascinated by what it tells us about how we deal with the future and the unknown.

Although managers span the entire range of Myers-Briggs styles, their leadership styles tend to fall in one of four categories. Some are clearly visionaries; they like to envision the future and base much of their thinking on their imagination. I call the leaders who fall into this category "the dreamers." Of the thousands of managers who I have worked with in seminars and project activities, about one-third fall into this category. Another third of the managers like to methodically get the job done, following rules and procedures most of the time. When these managers run into a problem, however, they are very motivated to find a solution and will work hard until they arrive at one. I've labeled these managers "the inventors," since necessity drives them to be creative. The remaining third seem to be divided among two other types. One group I call "the explorers" because they seem to enjoy wandering from the main path to investigate new alternatives and opportunities. The final group, which is usually the smallest of the four, are "the adventurers." These managers thrive on uncertainty and excitement and look at many aspects of their jobs as a journey into the unknown. Each of the four types of leaders can be very effective in their jobs, but each does it in a different way. By the way, you don't have to take the Myers-Briggs Behavioral Style Inventory to discover your own particular style of leadership. I suspect each of us can put ourselves into one (or more) of these four characterizations. Dreamers dream a lot, inventors solve problems, explorers search for opportunities, and adventurers like action. Which one is closest to your leadership style?

While it's interesting to examine our leadership and management styles from this perspective, it strikes me that this analysis can really assist us in the creation of captivating challenges. As we've seen, breakthroughs occur when there are compelling missions, and our responsibility as leaders is to create these for our people. What better inner voices to listen to than the plea of the inventor, the tale of the dreamer, the call of the explorer, or the shout of the adventurer? Isn't it this aspect of our being that gives us the motivation to excel as a manager and a leader? Then why not use these talents to motivate others? The inventor, the dreamer, the explorer, and the adventurer in each of us can serve as our guides in creating the challenges. They are also the parts of us that are captivated by these challenges. Fortunately, they are also present in each of our followers and will provide the same motivation to them that they do to us. Let's examine this approach to providing our teammates with challenges that they can't resist.

Think of the last time that you were really excited about achieving a significant personal or professional goal. Although potential monetary rewards might have played some part in the excitement, chances are that achievement and contribution were big motivators. Examine the event to see if either or both of these two drivers were acting on you. Now see if you can relate the drive to some part of your leadership personality. There's a high probability that you were acting in concert with one of the four inner personalities that we have been discussing. If the challenge had to be met before you could go on to other things, the inventor in you was at work. If the goal was part of a much bigger vision that you have about your life, the dreamer was likely responsible. If the fascination was generated by your need to go into areas into which others had not ventured, then the explorer was probably the culprit. And, if the challenge was exciting because it was different or interesting, then the adventurer in your mind urged you on.

If we are motivated by these characters within us, other people will be. Use your own inner mentors to energize your teams and organizations. Tap into your dreamer and craft the visions that will turn on the dreamer in your followers. Do the same with your inventor, explorer, and adventurer personalities. Let them provide the challenges that will captivate your followers. The richer the challenge, the more excitement it will generate; the broader the challenge, the more people it will captivate.

The National Aero-Space Plane project was both a tremendously difficult challenge as well as a very broad and complex goal. We began by attacking all aspects of the technology needed to produce the airplane. As soon as one objective was met, several other shortfalls moved to the top of the list. There was enough difficulty in this project to necessitate breakthroughs, and that's what we achieved. In addition, it appealed to all four of the characters of our personalities. It was certainly a dream of the future, it required numerous inventions, it was aimed at creating airplanes that would probe the unknown, and, for most of us, it was a great adventure. While all challenges may not be this broad or complex, we are all capable of creating challenges that will turn on our teams. Let the inventor, the dreamer, the explorer, and the adventurer in you be your guides. They will lead you and your teams to the breakthroughs.

Setting the Target

In aerospace terminology, creating a captivating challenge is like setting the target for the mission. Once the mission and the target are known, the pilot then goes through a checklist to make sure that he and his aircraft can reach the destination. Leaders might benefit from a similar checklist. Here's twenty-five high-Mach ideas to set you on the path to creating captivating challenges.

1. Find out what motivates your people by asking them why they chose their profession or career path.

2. Ask them what they do in their spare time. Given free choice, people will do what most satisfies their inner needs.

3. Interview your people to determine their most exciting experiences and why they were so exciting.

4. Ask them if they would characterize themselves as a dreamer, inventor, explorer, or adventurer.

5. Ask them who their heroes are. People's heroes tell you a lot about what they believe in.

6. If you prefer not to question or interview your team-mates, listen carefully to their conversations. People naturally talk about their dreams, hobbies, and heroes.

7. Give your people a test, like the Myers-Briggs, to determine, individually and collectively, what challenges would turn them on.

8. Read some books about breakthrough projects and decide how your project can fit the pattern.

9. Read some adventure stories outside of your field and see if there are any connections with your project.

10. Analyze your goals and objectives to determine if they embody aspects which can be turned into challenges.

11. Ask a personal friend, family member, or professional outsider to help you analyze your project for captivating challenges.

12. Integrate your goals and objectives into a larger vision and purpose.

13. Then, differentiate the vision into elements that would appeal to your team's inner motivations.

14. Break down your project into areas requiring invention, direction, exploration, and action.

15. Articulate the vision and purpose in order to capture the hearts of the dreamers.

16. Do it again, but now challenge the creativity of the inventors.

17. Once more for the explorers, and again for the adventurers.

18. See if the team is captivated by the challenge. Ask them.

19. Write a one-page, hard-sell advertisement about your project.

20. Imagine selling your team's project to Hollywood. What would you say or do?

21. If the energy level is still low, expand your goals and objectives. Take on more challenges until they are captivated. Why spend your time on mediocrity? Go for a breakthrough.

22. Assign your team the task of developing your project into a captivating challenge.

23. Force the inventors to invent, the dreamers to dream, etc.

24. Do whatever it takes to turn them on to the vision. Preach, entice, sell, harp, plead, cajole—do it honestly, but aim at their inner voices.

25. Then get out of their way.

The Second IDEA—Maintaining Open Focus

Leading Through Inspiring, Developing, Encouraging, and Allowing

Whenever people discuss the most extraordinary projects of their lives, two aspects of the experience are always mentioned. The first, which is usually the best remembered feature of the project, is the goal of the activity. The second, which most people find a bit more difficult to articulate, is related to the freedom, growth, and creativity that was experienced during the project. Somehow, the leader was able to provide the focus needed to meet the goal or objective, while maintaining an atmosphere which allowed risk-taking, trial and error, and excursions into new possibilities.

Over the years, I've collected more than 3,000 stories that describe people's most extraordinary projects. I call them breakthrough experiences in order to include those events that are less formal than projects and those activities that are not related to professional work. In the first chapter of this book, we discussed some of the key characteristics of these breakthrough experiences. While it's difficult to distill the list of characteristics down to just one key attribute, there does seem to be one concept which captures most of the flavor of these creative events. The critical concept is that of open focus because it lays the groundwork for the breakthrough. And nowhere is the role and behavior of the leader more important.

Open focus requires the leader to provide crystal clear direction while allowing a tremendous amount of flexibility. The leader must simultaneously channel the team towards the purpose of the effort while encouraging and even stimulating innovative departures from the normal path. He must juggle these two seemingly opposing thrusts while maintaining a team environment that will facilitate innovation. In examining the breakthrough experiences of others, four leadership behaviors appear to have been extremely important in achieving this open focus. While there are many ways to describe these characteristics, most of the breakthrough experience teams have agreed that the following four statements accurately reflect the pivotal tasks of their leaders: inspiring the spirit, developing the purpose, encouraging the synergy, and allowing the opportunity.

Since it's so closely aligned with creating the challenge, let's start with developing the purpose. In order for the team to focus on the goal, the purpose of the activity must be clearly understood. While it is important to describe what has to be accomplished, it is even more crucial for the team to understand why it is being done. Goals and objectives tell you what needs doing; purpose tells you why. Goals and objectives will stimulate solutions; purpose triggers a broader set of opportunities which, in turn, will expand the solution set. Clearly a goal of the NASP program was to develop an airplane that would fly into space. But the real purpose of the adventure was to provide a way for ordinary people to travel into space by using an affordable and flexible transportation system.

When you wrap purpose around the objectives, it leads to a much broader vision of the effort. Purpose is truly enhancing since it guides the team in achieving its goals at the same time it allows the team to aim at a much bigger target. The task of the leader is to develop the purpose of the activity, not alone, but in conjunction with his team. The team must really buy into the purpose of the project, or else it will just look like another objective or goal. Ownership of the purpose by all of the team is paramount, and the only way to accomplish this is to develop that purpose with the team. It's perfectly all right for the team to be given tasks and objectives, but they must be aligned with the purpose. And, since purpose is so critical, the team must feel an identity with it. The only way to do this is by painstakingly developing that sense of purpose with the team. Here, the leader may have to take a back seat to the team and act mainly as a facilitator or boundary manager during the development process. By leading in this way, a clear sense of purpose will be achieved which will be the basis for all the team's efforts, including the breakthroughs that will be generated.

Another ingredient of open focus is opportunity. The leader must orchestrate a scenario that provides every member of the team with multiple opportunities to contribute. Rather than tightly controlling all activities in the organization, the leader must broaden the responsibilities of his followers and empower his team with freedom. Although the team must be aimed at the goal, it should be given great latitude in choosing the path it takes to arrive at the end objective. Rigidly defining everyone's function and responsibility is fine if the goal can be achieved by routine means. If creativity and innovation are required, the leader must work as much on the openness as on the focus. And to do this, he must lead by allowing the opportunity.

It's critical for the leader to grant his team the right to try new things, to fail and not be punished, to venture into areas that are uncertain. Breakthrough leaders must say "yes" more often than "no," and they must be very open to new ideas and possibilities. The simplest analogy of the required behavior is that of the toddler's parents. After months of crawling, the young child will make his first attempt to walk. The first steps are usually very hesitant and falling to the floor happens quite often. For a while, the child may revert back to crawling, but, after a few more tries, walking becomes easier and is eventually adopted as the preferred method of getting from one place to the other. As every parent knows, once this happens, there's no stopping the child.

If parents do not allow this trial and error process to occur, the breakthrough of walking will be delayed for their children. Carried to an extreme, the toddler's growth will be retarded and the child's willingness and courage to attempt new innovations may be permanently affected. As with their children, breakthrough leaders have to allow their followers the opportunity to innovate. If the team's task is sufficiently challenging, there will be plenty of opportunities knocking at their door. The leader's job is to make sure that the team members are allowed to open that door and respond to the opportunities with creativity and innovation. Allowing the opportunity is a very important responsibility of the breakthrough leader.

Concerts provide an interesting metaphor for encouraging the synergy. Just before the beginning of a concert, most musicians spend a little time tuning their instruments. To those of us in the audience, the sounds are strange, even a bit comical. But we grow to accept this as a normal and necessary part of a concert. It always reminds me of how strange it would sound if the orchestra weren't coordinated and synchronized. As the leader takes his position, the musicians stop tuning and await the command to begin the concert. What follows is some fine music, full of harmony and rhythm, with everyone following the music sheets and the tempo set by the leader. Somewhere during the concert, however, there is usually a place, sometimes it's only a moment, that is very special. We can sense the power of the orchestra; we hear what is possible when everyone is doing their best and playing as a team. That is the moment of synergy, and it sometimes gives us goosebumps. While everyone in the orchestra contributes to this moment, it cannot be achieved without the encouragement of the leader. It happens when the leader brings out the best in his musicians, forcing them to go beyond the norm and add their unique contribution to the piece. Collectively, they make great music, a far cry from the earlier tuning-up noises.

When we reflect on a breakthrough experience of our own, the pictures that come into our mind are usually filled with the faces of people who we will never forget. Even the photographs that we take to remember these events are dominated by the people and not the products of the experience. The words that we use to convey the human aspects of the experience are collaboration, camaraderie, bonding, closeness, and teaming. Together, we accomplished the breakthrough, each person contributed, and, somehow, we made the impossible happen. After some analysis, the somehow usually comes down to synergy. Alone, we could not have reached the goal. Even together, it didn't look like we could pull it off. But somewhere along the way, we became more powerful than we ever thought that we could be, and that made the difference. It is synergy that allows most teams to break through the great barriers. By focusing our individual strengths on the task, the net result is much more powerful than the sum of the parts, and the collective energy of the team creates a resonance that can break down the walls.

Encouraging the synergy focuses the total strength of the team on the purpose to be achieved. Without synergy, it would be almost impossible for the team to achieve the breakthroughs. If the leader doesn't work very hard to encourage collaboration, coordination, and cooperation, it can also turn the other way. Dissonance, disagreement, and disaster follow when the strengths of the team members are allowed to conflict. The leader must try to understand the unique capabilities that each member of the team can contribute, determine how those capabilities can add to the team's performance, and encourage the synergistic application of those strengths by each of the team members. By approaching the team as if it were a group of musicians, each with very special capabilities, the leader can orchestrate a concert. But like a maestro, the leader must encourage this behavior. It will take time, practice, understanding, and patience, but the result will be some beautiful music.

Another aspect of open focus that the leader must strive to capture is the spirit of the experience. Open focus is like the flight of the seagull, the music of the jazzman, or the dance of the ballerina. It should be free and open, yet purposeful and directed. There should be exhilaration and excitement in the team. Long after it's over, the participants should not just recall the breakthrough; they should also remember the joy. There is a spirit which surrounds a breakthrough team, and it is again up to the leader to develop, encourage, and allow this spirit. Even more, the leader should inspire the spirit. No one person can make this happen, but the leader can really help by setting the stage for this kind of activity.

Once again, leaders must think of themselves as mentors rather than managers or supervisors. Like a maestro with an orchestra, a teacher with a pupil, or a coach with a team, the leader must work as hard on the spirit of the team as on their accomplishment of the task. Encouraging some excitement, allowing some fun, and developing some energy is all part of the process. Each leader will do it differently, but every leader should work hard at making it happen. For some leaders, it will be the most difficult part of their task since it does not seem to fit the normal way of doing business. But normal is not what we're after, and every opportunity should be taken to make this a part of the project. Inspiring the spirit will require some effort on the part of any leader, but the payoff is definitely worth the investment.

Choosing the Flight Path

Once the target has been set, the pilot must then determine the best way to reach the destination. That usually involves choosing a flight path, one that is focused on the objective but open enough to deal with unexpected turbulence, atmospheric changes, and other problems. Here's twenty-five navigation points to follow in choosing the flight path.

1. Have all members of the team describe their own version of the purpose of the team. Reconcile and/or integrate the differences.

2. As a team, go away from the work setting and wrestle with the team's true mission in life. Everyone should ask why the team really exists.

3. Assume that the team will be successful and try to guess the impact that your achievement will have ten years from now.

4. Is the team's mission or potential legacy sufficiently worthwhile? If not, redefine or expand the purpose to make it worthwhile.

5. Define the purpose broadly enough to allow flexibility and to stimulate creativity.

6. Get complete agreement by all team members on the purpose of the team. Take whatever time is necessary to achieve this consensus.

7. Take a hard look at the environment surrounding the team. Does it promote creativity? If not, change it—radically, if necessary.

8. Examine the rules and procedures that govern the team's operation to see if they can be relaxed. Routinely challenge these rules and procedures.

9. Set up a system that rewards initiative, even if the initiative results in failure.

10. Delegate as much authority as you possibly can. It's amazing how little you need to hold back if you really trust your people.

11. Become a boundary manager and protect your people from the system. Think of this as your #1 leadership task.

12. Set up self-directed work teams within the overall team. It's a simple, highly effective way to delegate authority to groups rather than to individuals.

13. Implement systems that promote innovative behavior. There are many benchmarks that you can utilize (see the references).

14. Get to know the special strengths of each member of your team by spending some personal time with them.

15. Use consensus decision making and encourage all of your people to do the same, as often as possible.

16. See if you can detect a rhythm in the team when things are going well. Understand it and attempt to recreate it whenever you can.

17. Go on an Outward Bound experience with the team. Prove to yourself that collaboration and cooperation can lead to amazing successes. Sometimes they can even result in survival.

18. If things are going well, try to capture and savor the moment. When things are going badly, work hard to change the mood.

19. Focus on the excitement of the project. Remind the team of what's at stake.

20. Praise and reward people for doing a good job. There are dozens of proven techniques, and the simplest seem to be the most effective. Put a gold star on their foreheads.

21. Enlist the high-energy people within the team to motivate the rest of the team.

22. Ask lots of "what-if" questions. They stimulate people's imagination and often lead to new paths.

23. Make the members of the team look like heroes to the rest of the organization. If they can't be made to look like heroes, make them look like pirates.

24. When everything is going wrong or when everyone is down, do something outrageous.

25. If all else fails, throw a party.

The Third IDEA—Synergizing Competitive Collaboration

Teaming the Intuitive, Directed, Evaluative, and Assertive

When Eskimos first tried to use dogs to pull their sleds across the snow, they ran into a serious problem. If four huskies were tied to a leash, each dog pulled in a different direction. The result was pandemonium and no forward motion. After experimenting with different dogs and various arrangements, they came up with a solution that has been used by their descendents for many generations. By carefully sequencing the dogs on the leash, with the strongest and oldest in the front and the youngest and weakest in the back, the dogs work as a team and pull in the same direction. The result is a very forceful team of dogs that use all of their energy to achieve a powerful forward thrust.

Energizing a team of people is a lot more complicated than getting dogs to pull a sled. The principles, however, are the same. Every individual has certain strengths, and carefully integrating those strengths can produce teams with exceptional capabilities. While huskies might be categorized by their size, strength, age, and energy, people are more complex. There are probably as many unique strengths as there are people. Nevertheless, a few characteristics appear to be more important in achieving breakthroughs than others. Specifically, there are four that seem to play a significant role in this context. While each of the four are needed to maximize the probability of a breakthrough, most people are usually strong in only one or two areas. The task, therefore, is to utilize the different strengths of each member of the team to achieve the goal.

In almost any group, there are some individuals who seem to operate from an intuitive standpoint. All of us are intuitive at times, but some people use intuitive thinking and intuitive reasoning more than others. There have been major personality studies conducted in this area, and there are several excellent books that examine the process of intuitive thinking. While almost anyone can develop their intuition through practice, some people come with a highly developed intuitive capability. Usually, these people are relatively easy to identify (you may be one yourself), and these individuals are generally strong contributors in the areas of idea generation and unique thinking. Highly intuitive individuals have a built-in sense for what is occurring without appealing to logical, deductive reasoning. Some of their thinking and decision making seems to come as much from their hearts or their gut as their head. They feel rather than think their way through problems, and they often extrapolate a very limited number of facts into a rather general projection. They tend to use and trust their imagination much more than people who require a wealth of data before making a decision. They have a heightened capability of predict-ing what might occur, and they are quite comfortable dealing with feelings rather than facts. While intuitive people may not possess all of these characteristics, many display two or three, so these folks are relatively easy to identify.

A second categorization involves people who have a strong visionary or conceptualization capability. These individuals synergize and assimilate information quite easily, and their focus is generally on a clearly defined and sometimes long-range pur-pose. As a matter of fact, they tend to have a difficult time oper-ating effectively unless they see the big picture or end result of the activity quite clearly. I call these people "directed" because their strength is to provide the team with a sense of direction either because they can visualize it or because they need it themselves before they can go on. The vision, mission, purpose, and goal of an activity are very important to them, and they will force a group to deal with plans and goals before they will commit to action. Often they are perceived as deliberate or contemplative, but they must understand where they are heading before they can move out. This takes time, and the delay can frustrate those who are eager to take immediate action.

The third broad category includes those individuals who are analytical, logical, and rational. These people tend to be orderly, structured, and categorical, at least in their thinking. They are masters at evaluating the scenario, deciding the correct solution to pursue, and applying a strong dose of logic to the situation. The evaluative characteristic helps us do the right thing; the evaluative team member helps the team pursue the best strategies and ap-proaches. Evaluative people are wonderful at analyzing the facts and data of a situation, but they are not comfortable making intuitive or snap decisions. At times, their interest in logic and analysis may seem a bit cold and calculating, but this strength allows them to provide an input that is not clouded by emotional-ism or over-reaction. Evaluative people need structure and organi-zation; they will force the group to consider deadlines, schedules, and orderly processes. You can identify evaluative individuals by their questions; they are usually asking questions like: when will this get done, where will we meet next, which is the best solution, how will we proceed, and what's the agenda for the meeting. By contrast, intuitive people are more into who and directed people want to know why.

The final category is made up of those people I call assertive. These are the ones who want to take action, who are eager to get on with the implementation, and who want to do something about the situation, now. They are impatient, they want to keep moving, and they want to act. Assertive individuals will keep pressure on the rest of the group and keep them moving along. If the intuitives are wandering too far afield, assertives will drive them back. If the directeds are spending too much time on philosophy and mission, aggressives will agitate for activity. If the evaluatives are into analysis paralysis, aggressives will force a decision. While their need for action keeps the team moving, total dominance by assertives will lead to chaos and confusion. Assertive people want to fix problems sometimes before they are well-defined. They want to try solutions sometimes before they're fully analyzed. They are the ready—fire—aim people, full of energy, excitement, and enthusiasm. Unlike the other three groups, sometimes the assertives don't even ask questions; they just do it. They are the spark of the team, often the leaders, and always ready for action. They're not hard to identify; they're usually in the front.

If you put intuitives, directeds, evaluatives, and assertives on the same team, interesting things will occur. There will definitely be competition: competition of ideas, competition of philosophies, and competition for time. The intuitives and the evaluatives will clash over decision processes, the directeds and the assertives will argue about schedules, and they all will disagree about the way to get the job done. It's inevitable that the four types will annoy and upset each other, at least some of the time. But this very competition of viewpoints can be used to generate breakthroughs. The clash of ideas, philosophies, and concepts is the very thing that leads to creative thoughts. Creativity only occurs when we or someone else question the way we have always done things. Conflict is often the basis for creativity. By using the competing forces of the team in a collaborative way, new approaches and paradigms will be generated. The team, as a whole, will begin to look at the situation in very new ways. Out of this collaborative competition can come synergistic concepts and, ultimately, break-throughs. Teams need different types of thinking to generate new ideas. The greater the range of thought, the bigger the potential breakthrough. Leaders should try to encourage and stimulate the wide diversity of thought that is characterized by the intuitive, the directed, the evaluative, and the assertive personalities. They should seek to construct their teams with people from each of the four categories described above. While some confrontation will result, it is the leader's job to channel that competition into collaboration. The result will be a synergy of ideas which may ultimately lead to a breakthrough.

Energizing the System

Once the flight plan has been accomplished, the pilot is ready to start the engines and energize the system. There are all kinds of check points that he now has to go through. Here's a few to get you going on energizing your team through competitive collaboration.

1. Find the intuitives on your team. Look for people who are imaginative, creative, mystical, psychic, emotional, curious, feeling, meditative, instinctive, and perceptive.

2. Find the directeds on your team. Look for people who are planners, dreamers, committed, questioning, re-flective, thoughtful, thinking, and conceptual.

3. Find the evaluatives on your team. Look for people who are logical, investigative, systematic, analytical, scientific, careful, independent, practical, loners, and detached.

4. Find the assertives on your team. Look for people who are aggressive, energetic, impatient, challenging, am-bitious, confident, directive, positive, and active.

5. Form four-person **IDEA** teams, made up of one intui-tive, one directed, one evaluative, and one assertive.

6. Use the **IDEA** teams to generate ideas, develop solu-tions, and examine processes.

7. Form other teams by mixing disciplines, like engineering, marketing, accounting, personnel, sales, and other functionals.

8. Mingle the senses of the team. Mix those who love art, music, sports, woodworking, reading, etc.

9. Combine the concepts and ideas that come from the different members of the team to obtain new ideas.

10. Have each member of the team look at the situation from another member's perspective.

11. Have everyone look at the same problem, but ask each team member to come up with a different solution.

12. Look for unusual settings, places, and scenarios that might lead your team to come up with new ideas.

13. Let nature be your guide. Take the team outside and see if the individual members can personally connect with nature and come up with new ideas.

14. Break out of the bonds of familiarity and look at your challenge in new ways.

15. Respect the hunches of the team members, as well as your own. They are based on individual intuition and rich backgrounds of unique experiences.

16. Change some of the members of a team when you feel that the team's creativity has dropped to a low level.

17. Use a pro/con analysis process when you need to come up with new approaches and initiatives.

18. Form integrated product teams made up of internal customers and suppliers.

19. Bring in people from outside your profession or field and let them stimulate your team.

20. Kids are the most creative people in the world. Use them to stimulate your team.

21. Focus the team on what they don't know rather than on what they do know.

22. Create mechanisms for the exchange of information across your organization's boundaries.

23. Encourage the team to apply new skills and approaches to the process.

24. Force idea generators, promoters, designers, implementers, and evaluators to interact and collaborate.

25. Take advantage of conflict situations; they can be turned into synergistic situations.

The Fourth IDEA—Developing Structured Flexibility

Fostering Intrapreneuring, Diversity, Experimentation, and "Adhocracy"

Edward de Bono, perhaps the greatest modern contributor to the science of creative thinking, has this simple definition of creativity: doing something that has always been done the same way, differently. De Bono has written over thirty books on the subject of creativity, but he has often stated that it all comes down to doing it differently: thinking differently, behaving differently, and living differently. People and their systems all too quickly adopt strategies and processes that suit the situation. As these behaviors continue to deliver positive results, they become habits and procedures, and they get etched into very strong human and organizational patterns. As long as things stay constant, these patterns serve us well. But if change is required, they become sources of tremendous resistance. If breakthroughs are required, these patterns are the very barriers that must be broken.

In most cases, the networks of habits, patterns, procedures, and processes are so powerful that they are extremely difficult to change. Think of how hard it is for you as an individual to modify an old habit. Something simple, like how you cut your food or how you catch a ball, becomes so ingrained that it takes great effort to change these behaviors. Greater changes, like major smoking, eating, sleeping, and working modifications, generally require deliberate and sustained concentration and, even then, often prove unsuccessful. Total lifestyle changes, such as marriage, switching careers, moving to another country, or returning to full-time schooling, are very big deals, and we only make these after a great deal of thought and usually with some trepidation.

Now think of how difficult it is for your organization or company to make a change in its procedures or general methods of doing business. Most organizations fight change as hard as they can. It usually takes a crisis or breakdown before any significant alteration is undertaken. The examples of American companies holding on to outdated procedures and philosophies, in spite of repeated and consistent signals to abandon them, are plentiful. Whole sectors of our economy and entire branches of our government are still mired in old habits despite the fact that the economic and political world has completely changed in the last decade.

It will always be difficult for people and organizations to change. To a certain extent, that's good because stability and structure are important to our well-being and effectiveness. But flexibility and spontaneity are also important, particularly where innovation and change are concerned. Fortunately, there is a way to facilitate the ability of people and organizations to change—build it into the system! If there is any real hope of breakthroughs from our people and our teams, the structures and systems that we set up must be elastic enough to allow change. They must, in the words of de Bono, permit us to think, behave, and live differently when it is necessary to do so. It is leadership's challenge to deliver the structure that any organism or organization needs for stability while providing the flexibility that will also allow needed changes. If managers create systems that provide this flexibility, then the job of future organization change-masters will be greatly simplified. If supervisors adopt an attitude that is tolerant of change and risk-taking, then their people will behave accordingly. If people and organizations live in an atmosphere that fosters and promotes flexibility and differences, then they will find it much easier to be adaptive and creative. There are many ways to do this. Here are four that seem to work quite well in fostering breakthroughs.

Intrapreneuring is a word coined by Gifford Pinchot in his book of the same name. He describes intrapreneurs as dreamers who do; people who take hands-on responsibility for creating innovation within a group or organization. The intrapreneur may or may not be the creator or inventor of the idea, but the intrapreneur is always the dreamer who figures out how to turn an idea into a profitable reality. With tongue in cheek, Pinchot defines the more common concept of the entrepreneur as someone who fills the role of the intrapreneur outside of the organization.

His concept is a simple one. If entrepreneuring works so well when people want to create something new outside of an organization, why not use a similar concept to start something new inside of an organization. Most people who start their own companies actually conceive the idea for the new venture while working in an organization that delivers a related product or process. They come up with a new way of doing what their organization has been doing for years, or they conceive of a new product that is related to some aspect of the organization's product line. Pinchot asks intrapreneurs to stay in the organization with their ideas while they encourage the organization to support the development of their ideas.

Borrowing from Pinchot, both the leader and the intrapreneur have rules that they must live by if the concept is to work. Intrapreneurs must be risk-takers, willing to be fired if the organization turns on them. They must be committed to their task, circumventing any actions aimed at stopping their progress. They must do whatever is necessary to get the job done and carefully surround themselves with people who will help them succeed. In order to circumvent the bureaucracy, working underground may be necessary. Intrapreneurs must also blend persistence with pragmatism and live by the rule that forgiveness, rather than permission, may be the easier to obtain.

Leaders who want to promote intrapreneuring should clearly state their vision of the future so that intrapreneurs can work on creating innovation that directly relates to the purpose and strategy of the team. They should seek out intrapreneurs throughout the organization, not just for their ideas but because these are the people who will implement new ideas. They should constantly search for ways to replace bureaucracy with responsibility, and they should reward intrapreneurs with new career paths that fit the special needs of intrapreneuring. Finally, they should make it clear that intrapreneuring, rather than maintaining the status quo, is the name of the game. Job security and job opportunity lie in becoming an intrapreneur.

A second approach that can be used to stimulate breakthroughs is to consciously and purposefully foster diversity. Bring in some new people, try some new approaches, create some controversy, shake up the system. The same old behavior will get you the same old result. One technique that we have used for years in the government is the blue team/red team approach. The blue team is tasked to solve the problem, and the red team is asked to critique the solution. Sometimes both teams are charged to solve the same problem, and the usually differing solutions are then debated and integrated. Another variant has the blue team developing the benefits that would accrue from a potential initiative while the red team analyzes the costs and disadvantages. Forcing the organization to look at itself from different viewpoints takes effort, but it generally produces some innovative results.

Diversity will also be a natural by-product of competitive collaboration. By utilizing the individual differences that are always present in organizations, exciting new procedures and processes can be developed. No two people will approach a situation in exactly the same way. While an underlying structure can serve to stabilize the team, giving people flexibility in their pursuit of the goal can yield a double benefit. First, novel and creative approaches will be developed. Secondly, each individual will be more committed and invested in the situation. We are all unique, and most of us like it that way. By letting everyone do a bit of "their own thing" within the broad boundaries of an organized approach, everyone, as well as the overall team, can be more creative.

Another way to achieve structured flexibility is through experimentation. If you knew exactly what was needed to achieve a breakthrough, the job would be simple. Unfortunately, you don't, so why not try many different approaches until you find one that works. But do it methodically. Start the process by departing slightly from the current strategy or organizational structure. Observe what happens. Better yet, measure the results. Use your observations and data to guide you in deciding the next experimental approach. Keep at it until you begin to achieve the results that you really want.

There are several major benefits to the experimental approach. The organization knows that departures from the norm will be the rule and that people must learn to be flexible. Since the leadership supports change, individuals will be more inclined to experiment and, thereby, try things that may lead to innovation. Since the changes are experimental, you can always return to the old approach without any loss of face. After all, it was only an experiment. Several small departures may yield a positive trend, and you might want to take more risks with the next step. Failures can be regarded as learning experiences rather than setbacks. And every experiment will yield valuable information that can be utilized at some later date when different results might be desired. Most importantly, experimentation will provide the team with the flexibility that it needs to circumvent the barriers which the underlying structure will inevitably produce.

The final recommendation in this area is the purposeful application of "adhocracy." Unless the organization or the team is extremely new or small, bureaucracy has already set in. This isn't so bad since some amount of structure and procedure is necessary in every viable operation. But bureaucracy rarely leads to breakthroughs. By superimposing some adhocracy on top of the bureaucracy, there's at least a fighting chance for innovation to occur. It's important not to drift totally into ad-hoc behavior, since this may result in more confusion than creativity. But some adhocracy will open things up. Set up some limited-duration, cross-functional teams. Create and acknowledge a second organizational structure that is orthogonal to the one that currently exists. Organize tiger teams to go after particular objectives. Push leadership down into the organization and allow people to circumvent the bureaucracy when it makes sense. That's the key to adhocratic approaches—use common sense.

If the structured system is getting in the way of good common sense, ad-hoc your way around it. If the reverse is true, go back to the old approaches. Neither pure bureaucracy nor pure adhocracy is the answer. How far to lean in either direction is very organizationally dependent. Large mature organizations will generally be quite bureaucratic, and leaders will have to fight hard to defend even small amounts of adhocracy. The opposite is true of small, new teams, where bureaucracy will be considered a dirty word. The trick is to produce structured flexibility, and it's the leader's call as to how much adhocracy is enough.

Working the Environment

With the engines fired up and the airplane ready to go, there's just one more thing to do before we take off. Every pilot has to get a good fix on the weather and the atmospheric conditions that will be encountered on the journey. Understanding the environment and having it work for you is a very important part of the flight. Here are twenty-five environmental fixes that should make the breakthrough trip more successful.

1. Encourage intrapreneuring by creating conditions that will allow intrapreneurs to succeed. Intrapreneurs appoint themselves to their role; it is the leader's responsibility to do things that will encourage them to do so.

2. Provide ways for intrapreneurs to stay with their "intraprises," even when policy gets in the way of doing that.

3. Let people do the job in their own way rather than have them constantly stop to explain their actions or ask for permission.

4. Create processes for intrapreneurs to access the resources that will be needed to try out new ideas. The procedures should be quick and informal.

5. Make sure your intrapreneurs are free to use the resources of outside organizations or other groups within the organization. Intrapreneurs live in a multi-option universe, and they must be supported in this manner.

6. Allow intrapreneurs to cross the boundaries of existing patterns in the organization. Defending turf and protecting "rice bowls" block innovation.

7. Develop ways for the team to try many small, experimental approaches to meeting the goal. It's better to try many times with less extensive preparations than to go for a single, very expensive attempt to hit a home run.

8. Encourage risk-taking and tolerate mistakes. You can't have one without the other.

9. Let people with solutions go out and look for places to use them. Defining a problem is sometimes a bigger breakthrough than developing a solution.

10. Give people the freedom to think. Idle minds sometimes produce devilishly good ideas.

11. Create openings for clandestine operations that could lead to innovative solutions.

12. Catalyze some solutions by building inexpensive prototypes. "Cut and try" techniques can be great learning experiences.

13. Try lots of things and work simultaneously on many fronts. If you generate a bunch of little sparks, one of them might just start a fire.

14. Create some internal competition to produce multiple approaches. Have two teams work on the same problem for a while. Merge them later to come up with additional solutions.

15. Formalize or allow bootlegging of resources, time, and ideas. Make it easy for people to get the help that they need.

16. Provide the team with an open, nonthreatening environment. Accept the failures that such a system will inevitably produce.

17. Eradicate killer phrases throughout the organization. Ban phrases like "Be practical," "It's not part of the job," "They won't go for it," and "We've never done it that way."

18. Regard any failure or false step as a learning opportunity.

19. Analyze the biggest mistakes that you or the team made during the past several years. What were their benefits? What did you discover? What new opportunities were created for the team?

20. Teach your team to look for opportunities rather than to solve problems.

21. Break some rules, particularly in how you view the project and the way you're organized.

22. Keep arrogance from clouding your assessment of the situation. Humility is an important creative thinking tool.

23. Challenge, discard, and destroy any assumption that gets in the way of achieving a breakthrough.

24. Although change is inevitable, everyone will resist it. Prepare yourself and the team for the inevitable battles ahead.

25. Loosen up—the team, the environment, the rules, yourself.

The Fifth IDEA—Nurturing Personal Commitment

Acting with Integrity, Direction, Empowerment, and Alignment

Committing to someone or something is probably the most powerful of all human endeavors. Usually, we reserve our commitment for very special things, like marriage, parenting, or very worthwhile causes. Even then, the conditions have to be right, and we must believe very strongly in the people that are associated with the commitment. If we can't identify with the people involved in a cause, then why would we support it? If we don't trust and respect our partners, then how can we subscribe to their dreams and objectives? If we can't grow and be fulfilled in our relationship with them, then why would we want to be a part of their team? There's no way to guarantee that any member of your team will commit to the mission or purpose of the effort. But you can increase the probability of their commitment through your actions. By acting with integrity, direction, empowerment, and alignment, you can provide your team with the very elements that most people require for commitment.

Repeated surveys of what people value most in a leader have consistently shown that integrity is very high on the list. To most of us, integrity is synonymous with honesty. We want a leader who will tell us the truth, who acts with principle, and who we can trust. No matter what television shows or movies have suggested, most of us try to live our lives around a set of values, and honesty is one of them. We all falter occasionally; sometimes we believe that it's okay to lie a little, and sometimes we bend and even break a rule or two. But most of us are basically honest, and we want a leader who is honest as well. We don't usually think much about this leadership requirement until it is violated. Once we find out that our leaders have lied to us, the trust is gone, and their effectiveness to lead us has been significantly impaired. Even our greatest heroes are tarnished when their honesty is questioned. If the allegations prove true, we might forgive them, but we find it hard to retain them as our heroes.

Breakthrough leaders must be honest; it's the only real way to get anyone to follow you. But they must be more than honest; they must act with integrity. What that really means is that the best leaders are integrated, with their causes, with themselves, and with their teams. While honesty is a natural consequence of acting with integrity, so are consistency and identity. By being integrated, leaders send out consistent signals. They are one with their cause and their team. If they are integrated, knowing their cause or their team should tell you a lot about them. The best leaders personify their causes, they bubble over when talking about their goals, and it's hard to think about the leader and the goal separately.

The best leaders exemplify their teams, and it's almost impossible not to see their mark on the behavior of the team. In the best cases, all three merge, and the team, the leader, and the cause cannot be separated. All three have taken on the same identity, and a commitment to one is synonymous with a commitment to all. These are the situations that lead to breakthroughs. By living with integrity, the leader can generate the kind of commitment that can lead to great things. It's not an easy task; it's more than just being honest. But the strong integration of the leader with the team and their cause is a very powerful leadership characteristic. With that kind of integrity, leaders can enlist their teams not just to follow them but to do whatever it takes to meet the challenge.

While integrity is highly valued as a leadership characteristic, there is another thing that leaders must do that is just as important. Leaders must lead! It seems so simple and obvious, but many managers and directors often forget about that fundamental task. Leaders take us to places that we have never been before, and that's why we follow them. They provide us with a sense of direction, a path that we can follow to our goal. If a leader clearly communicates the direction for the team to pursue and links that forcefully to the goal of the team, it's almost impossible not to follow him. Once people understand where you're heading and why you're going that way, they have a simple choice to make. As the saying goes, they can lead (with you), they can follow, or they can get out of the way. Unless they do the latter, they are committed to the path that you have set, and they will act accordingly. And if you pursue your direction with passion, they will follow you passionately.

I'm always fascinated by the tremendous power and influence that directed leaders have on their teams and organizations. Most people will search long and hard for a leader to get behind. Once they find one who is going in a direction that makes sense to them, they will jump on the bandwagon and follow that leader. Sometimes the leader's influence is so powerful that it's hard to get the team to change direction even when it's in its best interest. On the light side, we've all watched comedies where the field commander marches the band into a wall or the grandstand. There have also been great tragedies where powerful leaders have been blindly followed into terrible catastrophes and atrocities. While these illustrate the negative side of directed leadership, the same characteristic can be used in a positive way. If a leader provides a clear sense of purposeful direction, he has taken a giant step towards securing the commitment of his team. The more exciting the direction, the more energy it will generate. You don't have to be a rocket scientist to understand the force of directed energy, human or otherwise. Once people have made up their minds and have intensely committed to an endeavor, it's hard to stop them. The leader can play a major role in making this happen. In a sense, it's simply a matter of leading.

A third characteristic of breakthrough leadership centers around *empowerment*. While leaders can stimulate commitment through integrity and enlist commitment through direction, the team ultimately must take responsibility for its actions. The leader can model the way, but unless team members translate their commitment into action, the project will fail. And the only way that this can happen is if they are given the authority and responsibility to make it happen. They must feel that they have the power to take matters into their own hands, to come up with breakthrough solutions, and to deal with the obstacles between them and the goal. If they don't feel that they have the power, they won't act on their commitment. And they won't feel that they have the power unless they really do have the power. That's the essence of empowerment—giving the team all of the power that it needs to get the job done, even when it's a tough one that requires a breakthrough. Integrity and direction can lead to commitment, but empowerment will enable the team to act on that commitment.

Perhaps the best analogy regarding empowerment is, again, with the family. As a parent, you can guide your children and give them a sense of values. Sooner or later, however, you must let them go and see what they do. If you hold back on their freedom, they will always run back to you when they falter. But if you turn them loose and give them the freedom that they need to see it through, they will grow strong. They may fail at first, but they will gain confidence with every successful step. And as they grow strong and confident, they will become more committed to success.

Acting with integrity, direction, and empowerment can generate a strong sense of commitment from the team. There are countless examples where this has occurred. But what happens when things get rough and the team runs into resistance. That's where alignment comes in to shore up the team. By aligning the goals and the strengths of the team, the leader can prepare his team to better deal with this resistance. If everyone is lined up with the goal, it's going to be very difficult for anything to withstand the power of the team.

A single photon doesn't shed much light on the subject. You can create a more intense beam by generating a lot of photons and reflecting the light with a conical mirror. The beam will become even more powerful if you focus the light with a lens. If the lens is strong enough and the light is intense, you might even be able to burn a hole through some thin materials. But if you really want to bore through a thick barrier, generate all the light at the same frequency and amplify its energy through stimulated emission. That's the fundamental process of a laser, and we all know about the power of a laser. If you do the same thing with people, you might achieve the same result. Get them all on the same frequency through alignment, and the team will self-stimulate. Once that happens, there won't be many barriers that will be able to survive its force.

Applying the Force

With the engines at full power, the runway clear, and the weather cooperating, we're ready to take off on our flight. It's now a matter of applying the force, directing the thrust, and lifting off into the sky. Here are twenty-five high-powered ways to get you up into the wild blue yonder.

1. Become synonymous with your cause. Integrate yourself so totally with your goal that when people think of your goal, they automatically think of you.

2. Identify completely with your team. They are an extension of you, and you should be an extension of them.

3. Take time to work out your priorities, then let your leadership be consistent with them.

4. Share your dreams as well as your nightmares with your team.

5. Get to really know your team and let them really know who you are.

6. Be brutally honest with your team, particularly if you haven't always been.

7. Think of your team as your family.

8. Be as noble as you can be. How would your greatest hero or heroine act in your situation?

9. Give your team a clear sense of the direction that they must follow to meet the challenge.

10. Communicate your vision with passion. Communicate your direction with conviction.

11. Use imagery, metaphors, and pictures when talking about direction. It allows people to relate, and this can lead to stronger commitment.

12. Get the team's commitment before setting out on a major thrust towards the goal. Work hard and try to get everyone on board.

13. If some people can't commit to the goal or the direction, maybe they shouldn't be part of the team.

14. If you must change direction along the way to the goal, make sure everyone buys into the change.

15. Lead as if you know exactly where you're going, even when you're not absolutely sure.

16. Disburse your power to the team; grant them the ability to use your power to get things done.

17. Think of yourself at the bottom of the organization; that is, you work for the team.

18. Be prepared to go the limit for the sake of the team and the breakthrough.

19. Show the team what could happen, then give them the power to make it happen.

20. Make sure everyone is aiming in the same direction. Have everyone understand each member's true commitment.

21. Reinforce the team's power by making them take responsibility for the results.

22. Look for the common denominator that everyone can commit to.

23. Although change is inevitable, everyone will resist it. Prepare the team for the battles ahead by giving them the power to be victorious.

24. Keep your commitments simple and few. State them clearly and always be true to them.

25. Lead the way, but follow your team. Keep your word, but give away your power.

The Sixth IDEA—Producing Organized Adventure

Living with Intensity, Determination, Enthusiasm, and Abandon

Robert Frost, in one of his most famous poems, reveals that he took the road less traveled and that it made all the difference. Not too long ago, my wife reminded me of Frost's poem as we began our annual journey to open our summer house on Lake Waynoka. The lake is about eighty miles from our home in Dayton, and we close down the little A-frame cottage for several months because of the cold weather. The first trip is always an anxious event. Did the pipes freeze and break during the winter? Have the field mice set up housekeeping in our closets? More basically, will we still have a waterfront house or will the dam have broken? I load up the car to the roof with supplies and tools, and my main objective is to get there as fast as possible.

Since 1985, we have had two routes to choose from. The old way is a series of two-lane country roads that wind through seven little towns, none of which are big enough to mention. The other route, the new interstate, a divided four-lane highway, passes a mere four miles from our lake house. Because the old road is more geographically direct, it takes about the same time to get there as the interstate. But I always chose the highway because it's easier; I never have to stop for lights, and I never get stuck behind a tractor that only goes fifteen miles per hour. Since we make the round trip at least twenty times every year, it does get boring, and my wife usually reads or dozes during most of the trip

As we arrived at the turnoff to the highway, she suggested that we take the old road, just for the fun of it. I protested, arguing that it would take longer, that we might get delayed along the way, or that any number of terrible things might happen to my new car on the bumpy old road. "Where's your sense of adventure?" she said. "Aren't you the guy that flies at hypersonic speeds one minute and then roams the desert for two weeks just to see what's out there?" She had me, so we took the old road.

The normally two-hour trip ended up taking two days. We stopped six times to browse through old farmhouse antique shops, picked some fresh vegetables and had a picnic, decided to spend the night in an old inn that had just been renovated, and bought a wonderful old apple-peeler that we just couldn't live without. It really was a little adventure and we had a great time. We finally did get to the lake house, turned on the water (no broken pipes), swept the floors (no mouse motels), and then headed back to Dayton. I took the highway home that night and made great time—an hour-and-a-half. It was pretty boring though, and Marge slept all of the way.

Sometimes adventures just come along. That's great when it happens that way, but most of the time we have to organize them, at least a little. Just like my wife and the lake trip, it usually takes someone to convince you to start out on an adventure. Sometimes it's scary, sometimes it's uncomfortable, and sometimes it's just the fear of the unknown. While we all know that little adventures often lead to exciting happenings, most of us have to be stimulated before we will venture forth on this path. If we're on a team, we usually expect the leader to lead us into the adventure. And our response to the leader's challenge is very dependent on our confidence in his leadership, his attitude toward the adventure, and our expectations of what will happen to us during the adventure. If the leader is enthusiastic and confident, we feel much better about following him into the unknown. If the leader is courageous, a risk-taker, and lives with a sense of abandon, we know that the adventure will be exciting. If the leader is intense and determined, we can anticipate a novel and unique adventure, one that will expand our horizons and move us closer to the breakthrough goal. By living with intensity, determination, enthusiasm, and abandon, leaders can move their teams into great adventures. What's more, who wants to follow a leader who is timid, casual, cautious, and boring? Anyone can take the highway, turn on the cruise control, and follow the beaten track. But it's the less-traveled road that leads to adventure. Challenge your team to follow you down that path.

It doesn't take most of us very long to separate the really interesting people from the rest of the crowd. You walk into a room, and there's usually one or two people who stand out. They're intensely involved in the conversation, taking stands and stating their case. You might not agree with what they're saying, but it's much more fun to argue with them than to talk about the weather.

Their intensity draws you in, and their personal conviction raises your energy level. Even the conversation is an adventure, and before long, you feel connected to both them and their point of view. If their opinions are even reasonably close to yours, you can get pretty excited. And you just might be motivated enough to take some action around the subject.

Leaders who are intensely involved in their missions can generate the same kind of reaction. Passion and commitment are very visible, and leaders who display these characteristics have no trouble attracting a following. Everyone may not be willing to follow them, but there will always be some people who will. And they are the ones who are just as passionate about the possibilities. By living with intensity, you will be able to gather these soulmates around you and take them on a great adventure.

The next best thing to a passionate leader is a determined one. Most of us want to be with people who will go the extra mile, who will fight the good fight, and who will take us to the limit. You can pretty much bet that a really determined person will make things happen. The same is true of determined leaders. If you want to be where the action is, follow a leader who will not be satisfied until he reaches his goal. You can usually count on him to lead you into some kind of adventure on the way to the objective.

Leaders who demonstrate persistence, tenacity, and determination will bring out the same qualities in their followers. It's hard to be around people who won't take no for an answer without eventually saying yes. Most people have to be nudged, and occasionally pushed, into trying something new. I've always been able to come up with more logical reasons not to do something than to do it. Had it not been for some very determined people urging me to experiment, I would have missed most of the adventures of my life—even the little ones, like taking the old road to the lake, were at someone else's urging. This is an area where leaders can be tremendously influential. If you want to set your team on an adventure, lead the charge up the hill.

People will follow determined leaders into the most difficult situations simply because they trust that leader to keep moving forward. The greatest breakthroughs in most fields have not occurred because of inspiration or sudden genius; they have been the result of dogged determination and persistence. We all know that, sooner or later, leaders who demonstrate these qualities will shake things up and change the way things are happening. If we want to join them in their adventure, we'll follow them up the hill.

From the base of the canyon, however, steep hills can look mighty foreboding. Sometimes, there's a fine line between an exciting adventure and a perilous journey. Most of the time, though, it's all in the way you view the situation. If you look at it as a terrible burden, that's what it will turn out to be. But if you attack the obstacles with enthusiasm and excitement, even the difficulties can change into opportunities. The leader's enthusiasm can change a setback into an adjustment, a failure into a learning experience, and a trial into an adventure. And enthusiasm is catchy. After a while, the team will start looking at things with a more positive point of view.

How many times have we been drawn into something because of the positive attitude of the speaker? Everything that we do, both in our work and in our lives, is so much a matter of attitude. The most important prerequisite for creativity is attitude, a willingness to seek and accept change. And so it is with breakthroughs. A positive attitude can make all the difference in the world. If we are enthusiastic, it will foster the same positive attitudes in our people. It's very hard to be around someone who is enthusiastic without some of it affecting our own disposition. After a while, we begin looking at things in a more positive way, and the juices begin to flow.

But we're not just after a little bit of excitement; what we want to create is an adventure. So damn the torpedoes, full speed ahead. Throw yourself into the project with abandon. Lead your team like you were taking them on a crusade. Live your project as if the world depended on its success. Go for it, totally and passionately. If you do, there are only two possible outcomes. People will either run from you or they will follow you. If they run from you, it's either because they don't agree with your cause or they don't want to commit to that cause with enthusiasm. In either case, let them go and be happy that they're gone. Who needs people that are not enthusiastically committed to your mission? But if they follow you, they're ready for an adventure. Take them on it.

Taking the Journey

Finally, we're airborne, and the target is ahead of us. Eventually, we'll touch down, but for now, let's take the journey and make it an adventure. Here are twenty-five ways to make the journey as exciting and adventurous as possible.

1. Get passionate about your project. It's a dead giveaway that you really care about what you're doing.

2. Breakthroughs require you to tackle great problems head-on. Go at them with the intensity of an NFL linebacker.

3. Lead your team like you were leading them on a crusade.

4. Listen to the speeches of John F. Kennedy, Martin Luther King, Jr., Gandhi, Lincoln, and Churchill. Emulate their intensity in describing your adventure.

5. Pick out a few achievable objectives within your overall mission, and pursue those until you are successful.

6. Depict the challenges to your team's success as mountains to be scaled.

7. Characterize every small victory as one more step on the way to the goal.

8. Visually portray your progress so that everyone on the team will be aware of your end objectives as well as your current status.

9. Use measurable objectives to assess the team's performance. It allows everyone to quantitatively follow the progress of the team.

10. As much as possible, transform problems into opportunities. The more you do that, the more your team will look at difficult situations as intriguing possibilities.

11. Make your final goal the pot of gold at the end of the rainbow.

12. Think of your project as if it were some past adventure, like the Crusades, landing on the moon, discovering America, or climbing Mount Everest. Visualize yourself as King Arthur, Neil Armstrong, Columbus, or Edmund Hillary.

13. Throw your team into the situation, even if they're not ready for it. Fear and anxiety are legitimate aspects of an adventure, maybe the most exciting ones.

14. Live each day as if it were your last day with the team. Remind them often of the shared vision and the exciting adventure that they're living.

15. Stop fighting old battles and focus your team on new campaigns.

16. Take a few nonfatal risks. Show your team what it might be like to follow you.

17. Work hard at playing, and play hard at working.

18. Be enthusiastic about your project. Enthusiasm generates energy, and energy can explode into breakthroughs.

19. Be persistent. Never give up on achieving the ultimate goal of the project.

20. Throw yourself into the mission. Fall in love with your project. There's a hopeless romantic in all of us.

21. Think and talk of your project as if the world depended on its success.

22. Take time to celebrate the victories and acknowledge the setbacks.

23. Find ways to make fun out of work.

24. Use imagery and metaphors to capture the excitement of the project.

25. Go for it.

Making It Happen

Breakthroughs don't just happen like some flash of lightning in the sky. Breakthroughs occur because people make them happen. Like most other phenomena that are based on human behavior, their occurrence can never be absolutely predictable. But the probability of a breakthrough can be greatly enhanced by creating the right conditions. As we've seen, the conditions that lead to breakthroughs are a combination of captivating challenge, open focus, competitive collaboration, structured flexibility, personal commitment, and organized adventure. It follows, then, that if we can create these conditions for ourselves, our teams, and our organizations, then breakthroughs should occur. And that's where leadership is so important. It's the leader's task to set the conditions for breakthroughs to occur.

The first step is to create the conditions for yourself. Set some outrageous goals that are challenging enough to captivate all your energies. Focus your efforts on these goals, but give yourself the freedom that you need to get there. Supplement your strengths with those of old and new colleagues so that you will be able to meet the new challenges. Without abandoning your basic principles, take some risks, and open yourself up to needed changes. Commit, personally, professionally, and absolutely, to achieving the goals. Finally, make the achievement of these objectives one great adventure.

These things will not be easy to do. Changing the way we live our lives may be a breakthrough in itself. And sustaining that lifestyle may be even more challenging. After all, most of our lives are not one continuous string of breakthrough adventures. These times are exceptional, but they are certainly worth going after. If you open yourself up to the possibility of breakthroughs, they will

he great potential and the
project.

aches that might improve
o it.

am in planning and man-

ve always done things.

and on my fundamental
nciples.

t of our work.

in ways that make every-
ic.

dom in how they do their

elements of our team to

with new approaches to

the goals that the team

hat they are involved in

atisfy what really moti-

the norm in the pursuit

oster collaboration, con-
in the team.

follow. And so will other people. As a breakthrough leader, you can create the opportunity and environment for others to achieve their breakthroughs. Let the characteristics of breakthrough leadership be your guide, the IDEAs be your helpers, and your own experiences be your benchmarks.

> *Breakthrough experiences are the most exciting journeys of our lives. They take us into the future, into the worlds that we will create. They begin with captivating challenges, and the challenges become our destination. To get there, our flight must be fanciful and free, open to possibility yet focused on our vision of what might be. Our vehicle is not a starship but a synergism, the collaboration of competitive ideas. As we make our way towards the goal, we will encounter a new environment, sometimes structured, sometimes flexible. The force that propels us comes from within: our commitment to the cause. And the journey, if we are willing, will be an adventure. These are the features of our flight; a flight into the future, the final frontier of our minds. And, like the sky, the future has no limit.*

•••••••••••••••••••••••••••

1. I get my teammates to see
   exciting possibilities of ou

2. I look for interesting appro
   what we do and how we d

3. I involve everyone on the te
   aging our activities.

4. I challenge the way we ha

5. I let others know where I s
   professional beliefs and pri

6. I find ways to make fun ou

7. I articulate our future goals
   one on the team enthusias

8. I give my people a lot of free
   jobs.

9. I try to integrate the variou
   achieve synergy.

10. I experiment and take risks
    getting the job done.

11. I am determined to achieve
    has set.

12. I make my teammates feel t
    a critical project.

13. I work to understand and s
    vates my people.

14. I encourage departures from
    of our goals.

15. I search for opportunities to f
    sensus, and cooperation with

11. Make your final goal the pot of gold at the end of the rainbow.

12. Think of your project as if it were some past adventure, like the Crusades, landing on the moon, discovering America, or climbing Mount Everest. Visualize yourself as King Arthur, Neil Armstrong, Columbus, or Edmund Hillary.

13. Throw your team into the situation, even if they're not ready for it. Fear and anxiety are legitimate aspects of an adventure, maybe the most exciting ones.

14. Live each day as if it were your last day with the team. Remind them often of the shared vision and the exciting adventure that they're living.

15. Stop fighting old battles and focus your team on new campaigns.

16. Take a few nonfatal risks. Show your team what it might be like to follow you.

17. Work hard at playing, and play hard at working.

18. Be enthusiastic about your project. Enthusiasm generates energy, and energy can explode into breakthroughs.

19. Be persistent. Never give up on achieving the ultimate goal of the project.

20. Throw yourself into the mission. Fall in love with your project. There's a hopeless romantic in all of us.

21. Think and talk of your project as if the world depended on its success.

22. Take time to celebrate the victories and acknowledge the setbacks.

23. Find ways to make fun out of work.

24. Use imagery and metaphors to capture the excitement of the project.

25. Go for it.

Making It Happen

Breakthroughs don't just happen like some flash of lightning in the sky. Breakthroughs occur because people make them happen. Like most other phenomena that are based on human behavior, their occurrence can never be absolutely predictable. But the probability of a breakthrough can be greatly enhanced by creating the right conditions. As we've seen, the conditions that lead to breakthroughs are a combination of captivating challenge, open focus, competitive collaboration, structured flexibility, personal commitment, and organized adventure. It follows, then, that if we can create these conditions for ourselves, our teams, and our organizations, then breakthroughs should occur. And that's where leadership is so important. It's the leader's task to set the conditions for breakthroughs to occur.

The first step is to create the conditions for yourself. Set some outrageous goals that are challenging enough to captivate all your energies. Focus your efforts on these goals, but give yourself the freedom that you need to get there. Supplement your strengths with those of old and new colleagues so that you will be able to meet the new challenges. Without abandoning your basic principles, take some risks, and open yourself up to needed changes. Commit, personally, professionally, and absolutely, to achieving the goals. Finally, make the achievement of these objectives one great adventure.

These things will not be easy to do. Changing the way we live our lives may be a breakthrough in itself. And sustaining that lifestyle may be even more challenging. After all, most of our lives are not one continuous string of breakthrough adventures. These times are exceptional, but they are certainly worth going after. If you open yourself up to the possibility of breakthroughs, they will follow. And so will other people. As a breakthrough leader, you can create the opportunity and environment for others to achieve their breakthroughs. Let the characteristics of breakthrough leadership be your guide, the IDEAs be your helpers, and your own experiences be your benchmarks.

> *Breakthrough experiences are the most exciting journeys of our lives. They take us into the future, into the worlds that we will create. They begin with captivating challenges, and the challenges become our destination. To get there, our flight must be fanciful and free, open to possibility yet focused on our vision of what might be. Our vehicle is not a starship but a synergism, the collaboration of competitive ideas. As we make our way towards the goal, we will encounter a new environment, sometimes structured, sometimes flexible. The force that propels us comes from within: our commitment to the cause. And the journey, if we are willing, will be an adventure. These are the features of our flight; a flight into the future, the final frontier of our minds. And, like the sky, the future has no limit.*

● ●

APPENDIX

Innovation Development Effectiveness Assessment

The following thirty questions are provided so that you can examine your breakthrough leadership practices. Answer each question by scoring your behavior on the following seven-point scale.

1. I never behave that way.

2. I rarely behave that way.

3. I occasionally behave that way.

4. I sometimes behave that way.

5. I often behave that way.

6. I usually behave that way.

7. I always behave that way.

Use the score sheet that follows the assessment to record your answers.

1. I get my teammates to see the great potential and the exciting possibilities of our project.

2. I look for interesting approaches that might improve what we do and how we do it.

3. I involve everyone on the team in planning and managing our activities.

4. I challenge the way we have always done things.

5. I let others know where I stand on my fundamental professional beliefs and principles.

6. I find ways to make fun out of our work.

7. I articulate our future goals in ways that make everyone on the team enthusiastic.

8. I give my people a lot of freedom in how they do their jobs.

9. I try to integrate the various elements of our team to achieve synergy.

10. I experiment and take risks with new approaches to getting the job done.

11. I am determined to achieve the goals that the team has set.

12. I make my teammates feel that they are involved in a critical project.

13. I work to understand and satisfy what really motivates my people.

14. I encourage departures from the norm in the pursuit of our goals.

15. I search for opportunities to foster collaboration, consensus, and cooperation within the team.

Grove, Andrew S. *High Output Management*. New York: Random House, 1983.

Hagberg, Janet O. *Real Power: Stages of Personal Power in Organizations*. Minneapolis: Winston Press, 1984.

Handy, Charles. *The Age of Unreason*. Boston: Harvard Business School Press, 1989.

Heider, John. *The Tao of Leadership: Leadership Strategies for a New Age*. New York: Bantam Books, 1986.

Hitt, William D. *Management in Action: Guidelines for New Managers*. Columbus, OH: Battelle Press, 1984.

Jamison, Kaleel. *The Nibble Theory and the Kernel of Power*. New York: Paulist Press, 1984.

Kanter, Rosabeth Moss. *The Change Masters*. New York: Simon & Schuster, 1983.

Kelley, Robert E. *The Gold Collar Worker*. Reading, MA: Addison-Wesley, 1985.

Kiersey, David, and Marilyn Bates. *Please Understand Me: Character and Temperament Types*. Del Mar, CA: Prometheus Nemesis Book Company, 1978.

Kouzes, James M., and Barry Z. Posner, *The Leadership Challenge*. San Francisco, CA: Jossey-Bass, 1987.

Leavitt, Harold J. *Corporate Pathfinders*. Homewood, IL: Dow Jones-Irwin, 1986.

Magaziner, Ira, and Mark Patinkin. *The Silent War: Inside the Global Business Battles Shaping America's Future*. New York: Random House, 1989.

McCall, Morgan W. Jr., and Michael M. Lombardo, eds. *Leadership: Where Else Can We Go?* Durham, NC: Duke University Press, 1978.

McCormack, Mark H. *What They Don't Teach You at Harvard Business School*. New York: Bantam Books, 1984.

Miller, Lawrence M. *Barbarians to Bureaucrats: Corporate Life Cycle Strategies*. New York: Clarkson N. Potter, 1989.

Miller, William C. *The Creative Edge: Fostering Innovation Where You Work*. Reading, MA: Addison-Wesley, 1987.

Naisbitt, John. *Megatrends: Ten New Directions Transforming Our Lives*. New York: Warner Books, 1982.

Naisbitt, John, and Patricia Aburdene. *Re-Inventing the Corporation.* New York: Warner Books, 1985.

Neustadt, Richard E., and Ernest R. May. *Thinking in Time: The Uses of History for Decision Makers.* New York: The Free Press, 1986.

Osborn, A. F. *Applied Imagination: Principles and Procedures of Creative Problem Solving.* New York: Scribners, 1963.

Parnes, Sidney J. *The Magic of Your Mind.* Buffalo: Creative Education Foundation and Bearly Limited, 1981.

Paulus, Trina. *Hope for the Flowers.* New York: Paulist Press, 1972.

Peters, Tom. *Thriving on Chaos: Handbook for a Management Revolution.* New York: Alfred Knopf, 1987.

Peters, Tom, and Nancy Austin. *A Passion for Excellence: The Leadership Difference.* New York: Random House, 1985.

Peters, Tom, and Robert Waterman, Jr. *In Search of Excellence.* New York: Warner Books, 1982.

Pinchot, Gifford III. *Intrapreneuring.* New York: Harper & Row, 1985.

Ramey, David A. *Empowering Leaders.* Kansas City, MO: Sheed & Ward, 1991.

Roberts, Edward B., ed. *Generating Technological Innovation.* New York: Oxford University Press, 1987.

Savage, Charles M. *Fifth Generation Management.* Bedford, MA: Digital Press, 1990.

Stein, Morris I. *Stimulating Creativity*, vols. 1 and 2. New York: Academic Press, 1974.

Torrance, E. Paul. *The Search for Satori and Creativity.* Buffalo: The Creative Education Foundation and Bearly Limited, 1979.

von Oech, Roger. *A Kick in the Seat of the Pants.* New York: Harper & Row, 1986.

———. *A Whack on the Side of the Head.* Menlo Park, CA: Creative Think, 1982.

Westney, D. Eleanor. *Imitation and Innovation.* Cambridge, MA: Harvard University Press, 1987.

Wexley, Kenneth N., and Gary A. Yukl. *Organizational Behavior and Personnel Psychology.* Homewood, IL: Richard D. Irwin, 1977.

Winter. *Intuitions: Seeing with the Heart.* Norfolk, VA: The Donning Company, 1988.